# THE ANIMAL STYLE
# IN SOUTH RUSSIA
# AND CHINA

# The Animal Style in South Russia

and China

M. ROSTOVTZEFF

HACKER ART BOOKS
NEW YORK
1973

TO
THE MEMORY OF
N. P. KONDAKOV
AND
COUNT I. I. TOLSTOI

First published in Princeton, 1929 as Vol XIV of the
Princeton Monographs in Art and Archaeology
Reissued 1973 by
Hacker Art Books, Inc.
New York, New York
Library of Congress Catalogue Number 75-143361
ISBN 0-87817-080-4

Printed in the United States of America

# CONTENTS

# PREFACE

THE contents of this book formed the material of a course of lectures given in August 1925 at Princeton University, under the auspices of the Harvard-Princeton Fine Arts Club, to a small but select group of students in the History of Art. The lectures were made possible through the generosity of Mr. Otto Kahn. The concept embodied in these lectures was committed to writing and prepared for publication (*in Russian*) as early as 1921. This projected work was quoted in the bibliography of my book Iranians and Greeks in South Russia, *Oxford*, 1922, *but was never printed*. Habent sua fata libelli. *The Russian periodical for which it had been prepared, never appeared. This Russian work appears now in English, in an enlarged and remodeled form, because since writing the previous work, I have had the opportunity of seeing much new material, and have changed some of my views on the evolution of the animal style.*

*An old and good habit allows an author concluding his preface to thank those who have lightened the task of composing and illustrating his book. My thanks are due first of all to the Harvard-Princeton Fine Arts Club, under whose auspices this book is printed. The ungrateful task of reviewing my English has been undertaken in the most liberal spirit by Professor A. M. Friend, of Princeton, and Professor C. R. Morey, of the same University, whom I beg to accept my deepest thanks for their invaluable assistance. For photographs from which the plates are reproduced, I am indebted to the liberal help of many Institutions and private collectors: the Hermitage of St. Petersburg, the Academy of the History of Material Civilization of St. Petersbourg, the Metropolitan Museum of Art of New York, the Field Museum of Natural History of Chicago, the Archæological Administration of India, the British Museum, the Louvre,*

IX

# PREFACE

*the Museum of Berlin, the Museum of Budapest, the Museum of Sofia, and Mr. G. Eumorfopoulos, London, whose beautiful collection was open to me for this book as for many others ; Mrs. E. Meyer, of Washington ; Mr. L. Wannieck, of Paris, and Mr. C. T. Loo, of Paris. I ask all of them and those whom I may have forgotten to mention to accept my sincerest thanks.*

M. ROSTOVTZEFF

# LIST OF PLATES

# PLATES

## PLATES

# PLATES

2. *Bronze Yu of the late Chou period. Tokyo, Collection of Baron Sumitomo.*

3, 4. *Bronze standard tops in the form of a bell, late Chou period. Paris, C. T. Loo Collection.*

XXII. 1, 2. *Bronze Tsun of the Han period. Chicago, Art Institute.*

XXIII. 1. *Bronze spear-head of the late Chou or of the Han period. Philadelphia, Museum.*

2, 3. *Two bronze swords of the Scythian type. Paris, C. T. Loo Collection.*

4. *Bronze stirrups of the Han (?) period. Chicago, Field Museum.*

XXIV. 1. *Silk stuffs, a gold phalera, and a gold openwork plaque (inlaid), from Mongolian graves. Hermitage.*

XXIV A. 1, 2. *Wool stuffs from Mongolian graves. Hermitage.*

XXV. 1, 7. *Sarmatian bronze plaques from North China and Mongolia : 1, 2. New York, Metropolitan Museum ; 3, 4, 6. Wannieck Collection ; 5, 7. Paris, C. T. Loo Collection.*

XXVI. 1. 5. *Sarmation bronze plaques from North China and Mongolia : 1. Stockholm, Museum ; 2, 5. Paris, C. T. Loo Collection.*

# PLATES

# PLATES

# INTRODUCTION

## THE ANIMAL STYLE OUTSIDE OF SOUTH RUSSIA

THE history of the animal style in the decorative art of the ancient world has never been carefully and fully investigated. Special monographs have been devoted to one of its motives—the antithetic group.[1] In illustrating the development of the pottery of Susa, E. Pottier has endeavoured to show the influence of this ware, which has the animal decoration as one of its most prominent features, on later pottery both in Asia and in Europe.[2] Some general remarks have been occasionally made on the most prominent features of the animal style in South Russia.[3] And some scholars have drawn parallels between this animal style and the animal style of the early periods of mediaeval art.[4] As such, the animal style in its various local aspects and in its evolution has never been made the subject of a careful study.

It is not my intention to do it in this short book. Long years of study of South Russian antiquities have convinced me how very important such a comparative study of the animal style might be, both for the correct understanding of ancient art in general and of the beginnings of European art both in Western Europe and in Russia in particular. I have collected material on the question and have endeavoured to classify and to organize it. However, before such a general study could be presented to the historians of art, some special investigations and monographs are very much needed and one of them is offered in the present volume.

Let me begin with a short sketch of the evolution of the animal style outside of South Russia. Such a sketch though incomplete and general is indispensable for the understanding of this monograph. The general outlines of the evolution of the animal style as presented here are, of course, subject to modifications and alterations which may result from the increase of our knowledge and from a better classification of the available material in special monographs.

The animal style seems to be the oldest style in the decorative art of mankind. Whatever may be our ideas on the meaning of the late palaeolithic representations of animals, there is no doubt that the figures of animals were used in this period, both for religious and magical purposes and for decoration. This is shown by the figures of animals carved and engraved on various weapons and utensils of this period.[5] Whether or not there is any connecting link between these endeavours and the appearance of the animal style in the decoration both of pottery and of seals of the late neolithic period both in the Near East and in predynastic Egypt, we cannot say. We have too little information on the palæolithic period both in Central Asia and the Near East and in Africa. In Africa at least the figures of animals as a decorative motive seem to have been wide spread as early as the late periods of the palæolithic age and there is a strong presumption in favour of assuming a migration of these motives into the neolithic art of the predynastic period of Egypt.[6]

However this may be, it is an undisputed fact that while the neolithic period in Western Europe shows no interest in the figures of animals in its splendid decorative art which is purely geometric and abstract, in the East and in the South as well as in one part of Europe (the region of the Danube and the region of the Dnieper, the area of the painted and incised so-called Tripolje and related pottery), the animal plays an important part in the decorative art of the late neolithic times and of the copper age. The best instance is presented by the neolithic pottery of Susa and of the adjacent ruins and cemeteries and by the identical pottery of Mesopotamia. The pottery of Susa is, of course, geometric in its main aspect. However the geometric motives of this pottery are closely connected with animal motives, especially rows of animals all of one kind (goats, aquatic birds, etc.), and to a lesser extent with the figures of human beings. It seems evident that at least one part of the geometric ornaments, especially the spiral, represents the geometrization and stylization of animal forms. We meet a similar treatment of animal and human forms in Egypt also, though here there is an early tendency, probably inherited from the palæolithic ancestors of the early Egyptians, to treat the figures of men, animals and plants realistically and not ornamentally, and to combine them into groups and scenes illustrating the religious, social and economic life of Egypt.

Whether there existed an evolutionary link between the neolithic painted pottery of Susa and Babylonia and the later development of art both in Elam and Sumer is a question which cannot be solved. Pottier advocates a continuity of evolution at least for Susa, while Frankfort in his recent study insists upon a break of continuity between the first abstract and geometric style of Susa and the second naturalistic style of the same place, which, according to his theory, gave rise to the peculiar animal style which became characteristic of Sumerian art in the early periods of its history.

In the development of an early animal style Susa and Sumer do not stand alone. While animal motives are not common in the early painted pottery of Turkestan (Anau) and of many places in Central and Eastern Asia (including China), animal motives are on the other hand conspicuous both in the evolution of painted pottery of North Syria (of which one branch is the early Palestinian pottery) and in the late neolithic and early copper age pottery of one part of Eastern Europe (the Dnieper and Danube regions). The first region (North Syria) shows a well expressed inclination toward naturalism, being in this respect similar to predynastic Egypt. The second region presents unmistakable parallels to the evolution of the Susan pottery of the first style inasmuch as it delights in stylizing and geometrizing the figures of men and animals. A careful investigation of the so-called Tripolje pottery, not only from the point of view of its relation to the prehistoric art of the Aegean region but also in the light of the recent discoveries in Central Asia and in the Near East, has not as yet been presented. The problem is both difficult and fascinating.[7]

In the art of both Sumer and Elam of the third millenium B.C. the animal style assumes a new aspect and creates new and highly important motives. The most important new creations are : (1) the antithetic or heraldic group of animals, human beings, animals and plants: the group is often connected in the same abstract spirit with a stylized representation of mountains, rivers and buildings ; (2) the synthetic group of animals or human beings and animals showing a " symplegma, " i.e. an interwined group of two or more bodies in various combinations, the synthetic group being often treated heraldically ; (3) the symphony of animals : by this I do not mean the unconnected series of animals, but a sequence of men and animals all connected with each other either synthetically or antithetically ; (4) the use of animals and of parts of animals as tops, or handles, or bases of various objects : such are, e.g. the tops of standards showing the totem of a tribe, the bases of columns and poles in the form of a crouched animal, the handles of swords, knives, etc. ; (5) the shaping of some objects of daily use in the form of animal figures, the animal being represented mostly lying or crouched often with the head turned back ; (6) the invention of fantastic animals, i.e. combinations of various animals or of human beings and animals, the most prominent being : (a) the lion-griffon, i.e. head of a lion with ram's or goat's horns and a crest, and body of an eagle ; (b) the eagle-griffon, i.e. head of a crested and eared eagle and body of a lion; (c) the dragon, i.e. head of a snake or of a wolf-like being, with open mouth and large teeth, and with a crest and ears and body or extremities of a lion or an eagle; and (d) the various combinations of a human figure with the figure of a lion or a bull. The figures of the fantastic animals are used for the same purposes and in the same combinations as the figures of naturalistic animals.[8]

In Egypt, at the same period, we meet the same general tendencies, but nothing similar to the rich development which we have in Mesopotamia and which in that place was organically connected with the general development of art. This is the reason why many scholars would ascribe the parallel phenomena in Egyptian art to a Mesopotamian influence.[9]

It is still a problem how far the new development of the animal style in Elam and Mesopotamia was an organic development of the animal style of the prehistoric art. There is a possibility that the new motives were not created in the Elamitic mountains and the Mesopotamian plain, but were imported from somewhere else by new-comers, immigrants, such as the Sumerians, who probably came to settle in Mesopotamia in the early copper period.

However this may be, the new animal style as developed in Elam and Mesopotamia spread rapidly all over the Near East. The problem of the so-called Hittite art, even after the masterly analysis of Pottier, still awaits its solution.[10] The peculiar animal style of the Hittites might be ascribed to the influence of both Mesopotamian and Egyptian art, but might have been both developed from the motives of the early North Syrian art and imported by the Hittites into Asia Minor from their original home-land, where it might already have been influenced by the achievements of the Elamites and the Sumerians. Some of the features of the Hittite animal style are very primitive in comparison with the contemporary animal style of Mesopotamia ; some, such as the shaping of the extremities of some fantastic animals as heads of animals, are almost entirely unknown to Mesopotamia.[11]

The brilliant development of the drinking horn which ends in a body, protome or head of an animal, so typical in Asia Minor, Crete, Persia and South Russia, can be traced to the earliest times of Elamite art, but is almost entirely foreign to the Sumerians and the Babylonians (see PL. I, I). The popularity of the motive, both in Persia and in Asia Minor in the first millenium B.C. (PL. I, 2, 4), and the part which the animal rhyton played in the Minoan art might be explained by placing the origin of the motive somewhere on the Iranian plateau.[12]

The question of the development of the animal style in the Minoan world has never been fully investigated. The Minoan synthetic and antithetic (heraldic) group, so familiar to every one who has dealt with Minoan art, might have been introduced into the Minoan area from Asia Minor and be, therefore, a foreign element. The decoration of the swords of Zaffer-Papura and many of the engraved rings and gems remind one of Asia Minor rather than of Crete or of the Minoan mainland.[13]

Once started, the animal style never died out in Mesopotamia and in Asia Minor. Assyrian art took it over and developed all the peculiar features of it (see a selection of some typical articles on PL. II). It is very probable, however, that the rich development of the Assyrian animal style is due not to Mesopotamian traditions alone. Some motives might have come from Asia Minor, from the various parts of the Hittite Empire. Some others, however (the figures of a mountain goat as a pole-top, the open-work military standards, the popularity of a special form of the dragon, e. g. the wolf-dragon, etc.), are so similar to the motives of the South Russian animal style that a common origin is very probable.[14] The same holds good to a still larger extent for Persian art, especially for Persian toreutics and jewellery, as represented by the finds of Susa and of the Oxus (fourth and second centuries B.C.). Many elements here (e.g. the decorative use of a beak and eye of an eagle and of the tusk of an animal, the treatment of the extremities of an animal, the adornment of an animal's body by other animals, etc.), have certainly nothing to do with either the Babylonian or Assyrian traditions. We will come back later to this question.[15]

In Asia Minor, however, the animal style developed mostly on the Mesopotamian lines. The antithetic and synthetic groups are the dominating ones and are brilliantly developed especially by the Aeolian and Ionian Greeks. The chief fantastic animals of Mesopotamia found a new home in the Aeolian and Ionian art and were enriched by new creations. And yet, the decoration of the Ionian vases goes back to earlier motives. The plain rows of animals are again popular and reappear both in the common Asiatic art of the first millenium B.C. and in the contemporary and later art of Asia Minor. An analysis of the animal style in early Greek art has never been attempted, though it is one of the many fascinating subjects which require a careful examination. For our purpose it may suffice to state that the archaic Greek animal style, which survived in a few elements in classical Greek art and reappeared later in the Hellenistic period, was in the main a revival of the Mesopotamian animal style, in the form which was given to it by the decorative art of the early part of the first millenium B.C. to which we are accustomed to give the name of Phoenician art.[16]

The short outline of the history of the animal style which I have presented in this introductory chapter is of course a mere sketch, very incomplete and very meagre. However, the main lines of evolution of the animal style as traced here are based on monumental evidence and are probably accurate. They are indispensable for a treatment of the peculiar features of the animal style as they appear, simultaneously with the creation of the Greco-Oriental animal style, in South Russia.

# NOTES

## INTRODUCTION

1. E. Curtius in *Abhandl. d. Preuss. Ak.*, 1874, p. 79 ff., cf. *ibid.*, 1879 ; A. Riegl, *Stilfragen* 1893, p. 3 ff. ; A. Jolles in *Jahrb. d. d. Arch. Inst.*, 1904, p. 27 ff. ; A. Reichel in *Memnon*, 2 (1908), p. 33 ff. ; L. Curtius in *Sitzungsb. d. Bayrischen Akad.* ,1912, p. 1 ff. ; H. Frankfort, *Studies in Early Pottery of the Near East* : Mesopotamia, Syria and Egypt and their earliest Interrelations (*R. Anthr. Inst.*, Occasional papers, No 6), 1924, p. 121 ff.

2. M. Pézard et Edm. Pottier, *Antiquités de la Susiane*. Mission de J. de Morgan, Paris, 1913 ; Edm. Pottier, Délégation en Perse, *Mémoires*, VOL. XIII. The point of view of Pottier has been criticized by H. Frankfort, l.c. Frankfort denies a continuity between the first and the second style of painted pottery at Susa and any similarity between the early pottery of Susa and that of Egypt. Comp. V. Christian, Unterschungen zur Palaoethnologie des Orients in *Mitth. d'Anthrop. Ges. in Wien*, 55 (1925), p. 183 ff.

3. S. Reinach, *La représentation du galop*, in *Rev. Arch.*, 38 (1901), p. 27 ff., cf. *ibid.*, 37 (1900), p. 254 ff. (and as a separate book, Paris 1925, second edition) ; B. Farmakovskij in *Materials for the Arch. of S. Russia*, 34 (1913), p. 29 ff. ; E. H. Minns, *Scythians and Greeks*, p. 261, cf. Add. to p. 226 ; J. Strzygowski, *Die bildende Kunst des Ostens*, 1916, p. 27 ff. ; Zoltan V. Takacs in *Ostasiatische Zeitschrift*, 5 (1916), p. 138 ff. ; A. M. Tallgren, *Collection Tovostine des Antiquités préhistoriques de Minoussinsk*, Helsingfors, 1917, p. 9 and 66 ff. (and *La Pontide préscythique* in *Eurasia Septentrionalis Antiqua*, 2, 1926, p. 225) ; C. Schuchardt in *Berl. phil. Woch.*, 1919, p. 955 ff., and in *Jahrb. d. d. Arch. Inst.*, *Arch. Anz.*, 35 (1920), p 51 ff. ; H. Schmidt in *Jahrb. d. d. Arch. Inst.*, *Arch. Anz.*, 35 (1920), p. 42 ff. ; M. Rostovtzeff, *Iranians and Greeks*, 1922, p. 181 ff ; Gero V. Merhart, *Bronzezeit am Jenissei*, 1926, p. 151 ff. ; G. Boroffka in *Arch. Anz.*, 1926, p. 369 ff.

4. Hj. Appelgren-Kivalo, *Die Grundzüge des Skythisch-permischen Ornamentstiles*, in *Journ. de la Soc. Finl. d'Arch.*, 26 (1912) ; id., *Vogelkopf u. Hirsch als Ornamentsmotive in der Vorzeit Sibiriens*, in *Finnisch-Ungarische Forschungen* 12 (1912) ; id., in *Proceedings of the fifteenth Archæological Congress at Novgorod*, VOL. I (1914) ; id., in *Opuscula Archæologica O. Montelio dicata*, 1913 ; M. Rostovtzeff, *Iranians and Greeks in South Russia*, 1922; B. Brehm, *Der Ursprung der Germanischen Tierornamentik*, in J. Strzygowski's *Heidnisches und Christliches um das J.* 1000, 1926. My point of view has been recently supported by the careful analysis of the animal heads and animal-symphonies of Oseberg and Wendel by V. Schulz, *Tierkopfe mit tierverzierten Feldern im Oseberg und Wendel*, in *Mannus*, 17 (1925), p. 344 ff. It has been rejected by H. Shetelig in his recent book *Préhistoire de la Norvège*, 1926, p. 239 ff. I regret very much that Shetelig has not given himself the trouble of reading my books and articles and of studying the monuments more carefully. Had he done so, he would not identify my point of view with that of Strzygowski, nor have ground to wonder how monuments of the Scythian art of the fourth-third century B.C. could have influenced the style of the objects of Oseberg and Wendel. I have pointed out many times

and I repeat more in detail in this book my demonstration that it was not Scythian art, but the neo-animal style, one branch of the so-called Sarmatian art of the Roman Empire, which deeply influenced both the art of Northeastern Russia in the period of the late Empire, and also Scandinavian art. An interesting offshoot of the early Scythian (not of the Sarmatian) animal style is presented by the antiquities of the Avars found in masses in Hungary; Alfoldi, *Der Untergang der Romerherrschaft in Pannonien*, 1926, VOL. II, p. 13 ff.; N. Fettich, *Das Kunstgewerbe der Avarenzeit in Ungarn*, in *Archaeologia Hungarica*, 1927, VOL. I.; L. Matzulevich in *Seminarium Kondakovianum*, 1927, VOL. I, p. 141 ff.

5. On the "animal style" in the late palaeolithic art see H. Obermaier, *Fossil Man in Spain*, 1925, p. 210 ff., with an excellent bibliography which relieves me from the necessity of quoting other works on the same subject. I think it is not impossible to speak of the beginnings of an "animal style" in the palaeolithic art inasmuch as some of the features of the later animal styles are present at least in the Magdalenian period with its extensive use of animals and stylized animals and parts of animals for adorning some weapons and utensils : see Obermaier, l.c., p. 221, *fig.* 99. The stylized heads of animals are especially important and show striking similarities to later phenomena of the same kind. Equally interesting is the attempt to give to the tops of certain utensils (staffs and dart throwers) the form of heads of animals and men, Obermayer, l.c., p. 52, *fig.* 11, 3; p. 111, *fig.* 47; p. 128, *fig.* 58. Cf. V. Gordon Childe, *The Dawn of European Civilization*, 1925, p. 1 ff.

6. On the "Capsian" palaeolithic period and its art and on its influence, both on Spain and on Egypt see Obermaier, l.c., p. 202 ff., p. 257 ff. and bibliography on p. 411 ff., cf. V. Gordon Childe, l.c., p. 5 ff. On the earliest Egyptian pottery — H. Frankfort, *Studies in the Early Pottery*, etc., p. 93 ff., esp. p. 95, *Note 6*.

7. See the bibliography in *Note* 2 of this chapter; cf. V. Gordon Childe, l.c., p. 152 ff. and the works on the so-called Tripolje civilization quoted in his book. Cf. Ch. I, *Note* 1 of this book. We are expecting new and important information on the early stages of Sumerian life and art from the recent discoveries of early Sumerian antiquities at Harappa and Mohenjo-Daro in India ; see E. Mackay in *Journ. of the Royal Asiatic Society*, 1925, p. 697 ff.; Sir J. Marshall in *Arch. Survey of India, Ann. Report*, 1923-1924 (publ. 1926), p. 47 ff., P. XVII, c.d. ; XVIII, XIX, XX, XXI.

8. On the most important features of the Sumerian animal style see the article of L. Curtius quoted in *Note* 1 of this chapter. His treatment of the antithetic and synthetic group is a masterpiece of analysis. By *symphony of animals* I mean a composition where rows of connected animals cover the surface of the decorated object without interruption. The earliest example is the archaic mace-head of Tello, described by L. Heuzey (*Découvertes en Chaldée*, p. 233 ff.; PL. I *ter*, 2) as follows : " Le pourtour porte six lions qui se poursuivent ; chacun d'eux, dressé à demi, tient dans ses griffes la patte de derrière de celui qui le précède et le mord entre les épaules. Ils forment ainsi " une chaîne sans fin " parfaitement combinée pour la décoration d'un objet tournant. " An Egyptian imitation is the mace-head of Hierakonpolis (Egypt), see *Hieraconpolis*, VOL. I, PL. XIX, 6; cf. VOL. II, PL. XXIII. The same decorative idea treated in a realistic way is represented by the top of the famous Sume-

rian stele of the Vultures and by some other Sumerian sculptures which use the same motive. The treatment of a *handle* as an animal or as a synthetic or antithetic group of animals is best represented by the Sumerian knife, *Découvertes en Chaldée*, PL. VI *ter*, 2. The animals as *pole-tops*, both naturalistic and heraldic, used especially for standards, are familiar, both in Sumer (and Elam) and in Egypt from the earliest times : see for Sumer L. Heuzey in *Mon. et Mém. Piot*, 16, p. 14 ff.; and in *Nouvelles Fouilles de Tello*, p. 283 ff., PL. X, XI, esp. p. 290 ff., where the Egyptian parallels are quoted. Cf. the stele of the Vultures : the standards of the king and of the god and the animals of the chariot (reverse of the stele). Cf. also the sceptres of the various gods of Sumer, Elam and Babylonia : H. Prinz, *Altorientalische Symbolik*, 1915, p. 75 ff. Less known though quite familiar in the very primitive stages of artistic development is the use of animals as *bearers* of standards, columns and gods. The earliest examples are given by the Sumerian seals which represent animals supporting various symbols of Sumerian gods, see e.g. *Coll. de Clercq*, Nos 169, 173, 230, 232 *bis*, 234, and in other publications of Sumerian seals. The Sumerian seals are similar to the poles of Maïkop which emerge from massive figures of bulls. The parallels to these bulls have been collected by B. Farmakovski in *Mat. for the Arch. of Russia*, 34 (1914), p. 55. The same religious idea is embodied in the figures of *gods standing on animals* (Babylonian, Hittite, Assyrian, cf. H. Prinz, *Altorientalische Symbolik*, p. 92). An exhaustive treatment of the history of the *fantastic animals* in Oriental art does not exist. A catalogue by H. Prinz has been announced but not yet published, see E. Meyer in H. Prinz, *Altorientalische Symbolik*, 1915, p. 6. On the various forms of *griffons* see H. Prinz, s.v. *Greif* in Pauly-Wissowa, *R. E.* For the earliest examples of the lion-griffon on Sumerian seals cf. Delaporte, *Catalogue des cylindres orientaux de la Bibliothèque Nationale*, 1910, No 266, PL. XVIII, 266; H. Prinz, *Altorientalische Symbolik*, p. 74, PL. XIV, 3 ; p. 137 ff.; p. 144. Cf. Toscanne in *Rev. d'Assyriologie*, 13 (1916), p. 69 ff. ; F. Thureau-Dangin, *ibid.*, 21 (1924), p. 185 ff. The *serpent-griffon* or *dragon* : L. Heuzey, *Rev. d'Assyriologie*, 5, p. 129 ff. ; 6, p. 95 ff. ; *Les Origines orientales de l'Art*, 1915, p. 345 ff.; *Découvertes en Chaldée*, p. 234, PL. XLIV, 2. In Assyrian and late-Babylonian art the serpent-dragon is one of the most popular fantastic animals; note the upturned nose stylized as a spiral, Koldewey, *Excavations at Babylon*, *fig.* 21 and 32, and p. 221, *fig.* 135 ; Thureau-Dangin, l.c., p. 196, *fig.* Along with the serpent-dragon a wolf-dragon appears in the later Babylonian and Assyrian art with the same upturned nose. I cannot agree with Bossert (*Alt-Kreta*, 2nd ed., 1923, p. 17, No 55) that the crest of the eagle-griffon is an invention of the Minoan art, and from here migrated eastward finally to reach China in the Han period. The eagle-griffon with the peculiar crest appears rather late in the Minoan art. Like the other fantastic animals the eagle-griffon is a creation of the Sumero-Babylonian art and from this art was taken over by the Hittites. The Phœnician and early Greek art borrowed this figure not from Minoan but from Babylonian art. In Chinese art the eagle-griffon is earlier than the Han period, see Chapter III of this book. The history of the most Greek of the fantastic animals—the *Centaur*—has been recently written by P. Baur : *Centaurs in Ancient Art*, 1912. The type is no doubt of Oriental origin : see the various similar combinations on the sword-sheaths of

Kelermes and of Melgunov in South Russia, in the common Oriental style of the sixth century B.C.: M. Rostovtzeff, *Iranians and Greeks*, p. 52, PL. VIII, and E. Pridik in *Materials for the Arch. of Russia*, 31 (1911), PL. I, 3 and 4; and the *Babylonian parallels* in P. Baur, l.c., p. 2 f., cf.; Koldewey, *Excavations at Babylon*, p. 191, *fig.* 121.

9. On the status of this question see H. Frankfort, *Studies in the Early Pottery*, etc., p. 93 ff. and the article of V. Christian quoted in *Note* 2 of this Chapter.

10. E. Pottier in *Syria*, VOL. I ff.

11. *Ausgrabungen* in *Sendschirli*, VOL. III, PL. XXXIV, e; compare 206 e: figures of a griffon and Carchemish: Hogarth, *Carchemish*, VOL. I, 1914, PL. B. 14 a (sphinx, with tail ending in an eagle's head; cf. PL. N, 15 a). The same motive was borrowed from the Hittites both by the Etruscans and Samnites, and by the Haldians of the Southern Caucasus. For Etruria it is shown by bronze plaques which perhaps adorned shields; (R. Paribeni, in *Mon. Ant. d. Acc. dei Lincei*, 16, 1906, PL. II, 1, and p. 332; A. de Ridder, *Mus. du Louvre*, Cat. d. Pronze, II, n° 3450). For Samnium compare the constantly recurring motives of the Samnite armour (dragon with tail ending in a dragon's head, or an animal of like type composed of two foreparts of the same beast), which are almost identical with the motives of the Etruscan plaques (L. Mariani, *Mon. Ant. Lincei*, 10, 1901, p. 355 ff.; F. von Duhn, *Italische Graeberkunde*, VOL. I, 1924, p. 562; von Duhn remarks the great similarity of the fantastic animals of the Samnite armour to some animals of Celtic ornamental art). It is worthy of note that the same type of animal recurs in the finds of Mihalkovo and Dalj in Galicia; see M. Rostovtzeff, *Iranians and Greeks*, p. 226, note 6; cf. V. Parvan in *C. R. de l'Acad. d. Inscr.*, 1926, p. 87, and *Getica*, 1926, p. 332 ff. and 758 ff. PLS. XV, XVI, and A. M. Tallgren, *La Pontide préscythique*, 1926, p. 158 and 218 ff. For the Caucasus (the typical bronze belts with engraved animals, both real and fantastic) see B. Farmakovsky in *Mat. Arch. of Russia*, 34 (1914), p. 37 ff; A. Miller in *Bulletin of the Academy of the History of Material Civilization*, (1922), VOL. II, p. 287 ff. PLS. XXVIII, XXX. For a short time the motive of an animal with a tail ending in the head of another animal became fashionable in archaic Greece also; see e.g., the fibulae found at Argos, at Sparta and at Olympia; E. Norman Gardiner, *Olympia*, 1925, p. 93 f., *fig.* 18. In Asia Minor it created the well known Chimera, E. Poulsen, *Der Orient und die frühgriechische Kunst*, p. 107; L. Malten, *Bellerophontes* in *Jahrb. d. l.c. Arch. Inst.*, 40 (1925), p. 121. It is an important question, which cannot be dealt with here, whether the motive came to Europe from the Hittite lands or used to be a common feature of the pre-historic art of the Indo-Europeans in general. Common features in Hittite and early Scythian cultures have been noted repeatedly. Note, e.g., the peculiar standard-tops of Northern Syria and Cappadocia sometimes in the form of a bell with the figure of the Great Goddess and figures of animals, M. Rostovtzeff, *Iranians and Greeks*, p. 40, PL. II and V; *Revue des Arts Asiatiques*, I (1924), PL. III, Nos 4 and 6. Note also the similarity in the head-dress of the Hittite goddesses and women and that of the Scythian queens, M. Rostovtzeff in *Bulletin of the Archological Commission of Russia*, 63, p. 69 ff., and G. Boroffka in *Bulletin of the Academy of the History of material Civilization*, VOL. I (1921), p. 169 ff., and a general similarity of the Hittite and Scythian cos-

tumes of both men and women, a subject which requires a special study. Compare the typical Scythian and Hittite dagger which recurs in the peculiar Cretan statuette of Petsofa, F. Poulsen, *Der Orient und die frühgriechische Kunst*, p. 56, *fig.* 56, and p. 76. A close similarity between the antiquities of Van in the Southern Caucasus and those of the Hittites has been noted repeatedly : see B. Farmakovsky, l.c. and A.E. Cowley, *The Hittites*, 1924 p. 24 and *fig.* 25.

12. I cannot enter here into a detailed investigation of the history of the " rhyta " with protomes or heads of animals. The most recent studies on this subject, those of G. Karo in *Jahrb. d. d. Arch. Inst.*, 1911, p. 249 ff. ; R. Woolley in *Liverpool Annals of Archæology and Anthropology*, 10, PL. LXVIII, cf. *ibid.*, 7, PL. XXVII, Nos 15, 17, and 6, PL. XX, a ; H. Frankfort, l.c., p. 112 ; W. von Bissing in *Jahrb. d. d. Arch. Inst., Arch., Anz.*, 1924, p. 106 ff., point to an Anatolian origin of the rhyta with an animal's protome. However, a different origin is more probable. One of the most recent finds of Susa is a sacrificial basin of bitumen excavated in a very early stratum. It has been excellently restored (R. de Mecquenem in *Rev. d'Assyriol*, 19, 1922, *fig.* 6 ; cf. M. Pézard, *Cat. des Antiquités de la Susiane*, p. 102, No 224 *bis*). This basin shows a peculiar combination of three rhyta, with protomes of mountain goats (the body of the rhyton being the body of the goat), and of a ritual basin, the rhyta serving as the legs of the tripod (see PL. I, 1). There is no doubt that this monument is much earlier than other known examples of rhyta with protomes (two examples of much later date from North Syria now in the Louvre, PL. I, 2 and 3) and points to a Central-Asiatic origin for the motif. On the Minoan rhyta see Sir Arthur Evans in *Archæologia*, 65 (1913-1914), p. 79 ff. On PL. I, 4 I have reproduced a little known monument from Edessa now in the Museum at Naples. It shows the same style as the rhyta of the Louvre, the handles of the large amphora from Armenia (Paris and Berlin), and the rhyton of the Semibratnij Kurgan (Rostovtzeff, *Iranians and Greeks*, PL. XII).

13. See the bibliography quoted in *Note 1*.

14. A special investigation of the peculiarities of Assyrian life and art from the comparative point of view is greatly needed. The fact that Assyrian art owes very much to so-called Hittite art points to one peculiarity of Assyrian art only. The wonderful realism of Assyrian work, especially in the treatment of animals with a note of the pathetic and the tragic, cannot be explained either by the development of Babylonian traditions on Assyrian soil or by the influence of Asia Minor. It was inherited partly from the Assyrians by the Persians and was revived by the Sarmatians. It might be of Iranian origin. On problems of Assyrian life see A. T. Olmstead, *History of Assyria*, 1923, and B. Meissner, *Babylonien und Assyrien*, VOLS. I, II (1920-1924) ; on Assyrian art, see C. Frank, *Babylonisch-Assyriche Kunst*, 1922, and B. Meissner, l.c., VOL. I, p. 228 ff. Such features of Assyrian life as the horse trappings, the standards, the architecture of the tents, are not direct developments either of Babylonian or of Hittite life. On PL. II, I publish some articles of Assyrian workmanship which show some of the most important motives of the animal style in full development : (1) a brazier from the Louvre : note the stag-head as the handle-top ; (2) and (4) swordhilts of bone in the Louvre ; gradual geometrizing of the symplegma of a lion killing a goat ;

(3) a bronze bowl in the British Museum showing a symphony of animals; (5) top of an indeterminate article (bone; British Museum).

15. An excellent treatment of Persian art with a careful selection of the most important monuments has been recently given by F. Sarre, *Die Kunst des alten Persien*, 1922 (in German and French); cf. O. M. Dalton, *The Treasure of the Oxus*, 2nd ed., 1926.

16. E. Buschor, *Greek Vase-Painting*, 1921, may supply a general idea of the evolution as regards the Greek vases. Interesting material has been collected from a different point of view by Morin-Jean, *Dessin des animaux en Grèce d'après les vases peints*, 1911. See also Karl Friis Johansen, *Les vases sicyoniens*, 1923, p. 128 ff.; cf. H. Thiersch, *Tyrrhenische Amphoren*, p. 86 ff.

# CHAPTER I

## THE ANIMAL STYLE IN SOUTH RUSSIA
### THE SCYTHIAN PERIOD

I T is in quite a new form that the animal style appears in South
Russia. We first find this style in its most elaborate form, free
from any notable influence from outside, in the graves of South
Russia of the seventh and the sixth centuries B.C. There are no
connecting links between the civilization of which one of the leading
features is this style, and the earlier archaeological material of South
Russia. These *earlier* finds in this vast area (comprising the prairies
of the Northern shores of the Black and Caspian Seas and those to
the North of the Caucasus, from the river Ural in the East to the
Danube in the West) which have any connection with the evolution
of the animal style, are separated from the monuments of the seventh
and sixth centuries B.C. by many hundreds of years, and no one
artistic motive in them can be regarded as a source of inspiration
for the peculiar animal style of these later periods.

The finds of the earlier period which I have in mind are those of
the Dnieper region made in neolithic and copper age settlements and
graves, those of the Kuban region in the Northern Caucasus which
begin in the copper age and those made in graves of South Russia
of the earlier and later bronze age. The first are characterized by
the typical incised and painted pottery, similar to, but in no way
identical with the pottery of Susa mentioned above, and by some
beginnings of plastic arts—clay figures of men and animals and some
models of houses and of pieces of furniture. In the pottery of this area
the geometric motives predominate, the floral and animal motives
being subsidiary, either survivals or new creations of the artists who
incised or painted this pottery. The treatment of these motives is not
naturalistic, but tends towards geometrization, just as in the pottery
of Susa. This so-called " Tripolje " style lasted for some centuries,

influenced the contemporary pottery of the nomads who lived at the same time in the eastern part of the steppes of South Russia, but later disappeared completely without having left any notable traces in the later development, either of South Russia or of the Balkan Peninsula. The date of this peculiar civilization cannot be determined with full certainty. It cannot be later however than the beginnings of the second millenium B.C.

The Kuban finds[2] are an offshoot of a civilization which with its peculiar pottery and its battle-axes spread far and wide into Central Russia and Western Europe. It seems to be a civilization of nomadic peoples. It reached its climax in the Kuban area, where, along with the usual pots and weapons, it produced some marvellous creations of an art which in its main features was very similar to the earliest art of Elam and Babylonia and of Egypt. The animal figures are used extensively for adorning primitive gold and silver vessels and objects of the funerary ritual (the funerary canopies, diadems, etc.). The art is naturalistic, with no tendency to stylization. Attempts are made, just as in Elam and Babylonia and in Egypt, to represent the animals in their natural settings: mountains, trees, rivers. Elaborate floral ornaments are used along with the animal motives.

The question of the date of this civilization cannot be definitely settled. I was formerly inclined to date the copper age in the Caucasus in the end of the third millenium B.C. My date was based on the stylistic affinities of the best products of this civilization with the early art of the Sumerians and Egyptians,—the art of the protodynastic periods in both lands. Although the artistic objects of this civilization were certainly made in the Kuban region, we cannot discard the idea that they nevertheless experienced a strong influence from Sumerian art and that it was this influence which produced the short-lived blossom of a North Caucasian art. If so the dates of the mother and of the daughter art must be very near to each other. Later evolution in Sumer created new forms, a new technique, completely new devices of which we find not the faintest trace in the finds of the Kuban region. On the other hand Farmakovski suggested a much later date—about 1500 B.C. He based his statement on some affinities between the best things of the Kuban with early Hittite art. I still think that these affinities are illusory and must be explained by a common source of inspiration. We know very little of the origin and the earliest period of the so-called Hittite art which in fact is not a unit and has many and various aspects. A third date has been suggested by Tallgren.[3] Starting from a careful investigation of the pottery and of the peculiar forms of weapons and utensils he is inclined to date the Kuban civilization about 1700-1500 B.C. Whatever date we accept, even the date of Farmakovski, there is no transition between the Kuban civilization and the civilization of South Russia of the seventh and sixth centuries B.C. There is a wide chronological gap between the two civilizations, a gap of many centuries. Further discoveries might link up the common articles which were used by the dwellers on the Kuban in the copper age and those which were used in Central and South Russia in the iron age, but there is no hope of finding any connecting links between the art of the Kuban of the copper age and that of the men for whom the graves of the seventh and sixth centuries were built.

Closely connected with this peculiar civilization is the civilization of the steppes of South Russia in the bronze age as represented by finds both in the tumuli-graves of this period and in numerous deposits. This civilization is almost wholly geometric. The objects decorated with animal motives are rare and probably of foreign origin. These animal motives, as in the finds of Mihalkovo, Dalj, Pasachioi and Fokoru, show a close affinity with the animal style of the late bronze and early iron period in the Caucasus and Trans-Caucasia (Koban), and it is worthy of note that some genuine products of the Caucasian style were imported into South Russia (the find from Podgoritza near Kiev and an axe from Kerch, now in the British Museum). The animal style of the Caucasus is very peculiar indeed. It is certainly connected with the Hittite animal style, but shows at the same time a strong tendency toward geometrizing the Hittite animal motives and toward using them more extensively than did the Hittites themselves. Whether the Koban civilization is or is not connected with the Cimmerians and whether we may identify the Cimmerians with the people who lived a settled agricultural life in the steppes of South Russia in the bronze age, is an open question. In any case, the bronze age of South Russia and even the early iron age of Koban are separated from the seventh and sixth centuries B.C. by many centuries, and the peculiar animal style of this period as described below shows but few points of contact either with Mihalkovo or with Koban.[4]

This art, the art of the seventh and sixth centuries B.C., appears, as will be shown later, almost all at once, with all its peculiarities and without any preparation, without any precedents in South Russia : — a highly elaborate ornamental animal style, which certainly had had behind it centuries of evolution at the time when it appeared in South Russia. It is evident that this evolution did not take place in Russia. After the two brilliant episodes which I have described above, South Russia had but little importance in the artistic life of mankind. For centuries, in the long period of the bronze age, South Russia did not produce any notable monuments. The bronze age in South Russia is poor and unoriginal, and so is the early iron age.

Thus quite suddenly at the end of the seventh century South Russia was flooded by an enormous wealth of highly artistic articles with a peculiar and original style of decoration. There is no doubt that this flood came from outside. Whence we shall see later. I must however emphasize that we know perfectly well who were the bearers of this wealth and the agents of this new artistic development. Our historical evidence shows that a little earlier than the seventh century, probably in the eighth century, South Russia was conquered by a group of nomadic hordes, who destroyed the Empire of the Cimmerians. The latter had established themselves there some centuries earlier, but had left no notable traces in the archæology of South Russia. They were driven out or enslaved by the new masters of the country.

The Scythians are well known to the history of the ancient world.[5] The earliest writers of Greece know them; they are often mentioned in the Assyrian annals and in the Bible. It is well known that Herodotus gave a detailed description of their vast and strong Empire, which in the sixth and fifth centuries was a rival of Persia and the suzerain of the Greek colonies of the Northern shore of the Black Sea. The Scythians remained the masters of South Russia for a long time, from the eighth to the third century B.C. From the fourth century B.C. on they were gradually hard pressed and later conquered by a set of tribes to which the Greeks gave the name of Sarmatians. At the end of the fourth century, all the steppes to the East of the river Don were in the hands of these new-comers from the East. In the second century the Sarmatians advanced as far as the river Dnieper. At the same time the Scythians were driven out from the Balkan peninsula, first by the Celts and later by the Thracians. In the time of the Roman Empire they disappeared from the steppes of South Russia completely, being absorbed by the Sarmatians, but retained for a few centuries the steppes of the Crimea only and for a still shorter time the plain near the mouth of the Danube: the Dobrudsha.

There is no doubt that the Scythians were almost pure Iranians with a slight admixture of Mongolian (or Turkish?) elements. The scanty remains of their language show this with almost full certainty, and there is no proof whatever for their Mongolian, Turkish or Finno-Ugrish origin.[6] During their stay in South Russia they formed a strong state, with a dominating group of armed equestrians at the head, who were organized efficiently on military lines and kept their original nomadic life. This group recognized one king as the head of all the Scythian tribes, each of which had its separate kinglet and prince. In their prime (fifth and fourth centuries B.C.) the Scythians were the masters of all the peoples and tribes of South Russia from the Volga or perhaps the Ural to the Bug, and of a large part of the Danubian region. They were in constant relations with the Greek world through their vassals, the Greek cities of the northern shore of the Black Sea, and carried on an important trade with the Greeks of Asia Minor and the Balkan peninsula, exporting large quantities of fish, grain, hides, furs and slaves.

Such are the short outlines of the history of the Scythians. Now, precisely to the time of the Scythian domination in South Russia belong scores, if not hundreds of well-dated rich princely graves which were excavated by Russian archaeologists and which are scattered all over the steppes of South Russia. Larger and richer groups of them are concentrated on the Kuban river, on the middle Don, on the middle Dnieper, between the lower Don and the lower Dnieper, and in the Crimea. Scattered graves were found both to the East as far as the river Ural, and to the West as far as Bulgaria, Hungary and Prussia. All these graves were dug in the virgin soil before the burial took place, and a larger or smaller barrow was built over the grave after the funeral ritual had been performed. All the graves show the same funeral ritual. The graves are those of nomads : kings, kinglets, princes and chieftains. More modest graves were built for plain mortals, the common members of the tribe. The native conquered population was buried in plain and primitive graves of a different type. In all the graves which had not been robbed soon after the burial, was found a wealth of precious arms, weapons, utensils of a sacrificial character, jewels, adornments of clothes, carpets, etc. There was a fabulous profusion of gold and silver in all of them, bronze being used only for common utensils, for adornment of funeral chariots and for horse-trappings, and iron for arms and weapons and for the skeleton of the chariots. As a rule, however, even some of the horse trappings were made of solid gold or silver, and the arms and weapons were covered with gold.

The burial ritual was savage and primitive. In an imposing funeral procession the deceased was brought on a funeral chariot to the place of his eternal rest. Horses (sometimes scores or even hundreds of them) and other animals were sacrificed over the grave, including the chargers of the deceased and the horses of the funeral chariot. The deceased was accompanied in his grave by his wife and some of his servants. All that he needed in the future life was stored in his grave. Meat in large quantities in big Asiatic cauldrons, wine and olive oil in scores of large Greek jars, insignia of his power, (sceptres, axes, etc.) his best arms and weapons, his best dresses, vessels for food and wine and sacrificial vessels, etc.

The date of these graves (the series, as we shall see later, begins with the end of the seventh century and ends with the third century B.C.) and the fact that the ritual almost exactly corresponds to the Scythian ritual as described by Herodotus in his well known passage of the fourth book, leaves no doubt that the graves belonged to the Scythian masters of the steppes of South Russia and suzerains of the Black Sea Greek cities. If we happen to find in these graves objects, which are decorated in a peculiar style and which cannot be explained as import or imitation, we may safely say that we have struck an art which must be called Scythian art.

Let us therefore examine more closely the inventory of the hundreds of Scythian graves discovered heretofore. As most of them contain imported articles of Greek or oriental workmanship (no coins) and especially Greek painted vases, and as it is easy to compare those which did not yield such articles with the dated ones, we are able to date almost every grave and to attempt not only a general characterization of them, but also a division in subperiods. It is not probable *a priori* that the life and art of the Scythians would remain unchanged for centuries, in spite of changing political conditions and the ever increasing influence of Greek civilization.

In investigating the gradual evolution of Scythian life and art I succeeded in separating four periods in the history of Scythian civilization, each of them marked by some peculiar features, in spite of the fact that in the main the life and art of the Scythians remained stable in its main essence.[7] These periods are :

A. the end of the seventh, the sixth and the beginning of the fifth centuries, which I call the Archaic period;
B. the fifth and the early fourth centuries, which I call the Transitional or the Perso-Ionian period;
C. the fourth century, which I call the classic epoch or the Panticapaean period : a period of the highest bloom of Scythian prosperity; and
D. the end of the fourth and the beginning of the third centuries, which is a period of decay and of some entirely new features and influences.

Let me take all these periods one after another. The first period is represented by rather few graves. The earliest are :

(1) a grave in the Crimea on the Temirgora and another on the Taman peninsula, both dated by Ionian (Rhodian) vases of the seventh century. I reproduce on PL. VI, 3, 4, two bronze pendants ( ?) of the grave of Temirgora; one is the form of a curled eagle-griffon, the other is the form of an eagle-griffon's head. On PL. VI, 5, is a bronze ornament from the Taman peninsula in the form of two heraldic lions;

(2) a comparatively large group of graves in the Kuban region, dated, some of them, by Greek imported articles in the sixth century B.C., some by similar Greek articles in the very beginning of the fifth century; the best and richest representatives of this group are the barrow-graves of Kelermes, the graves near the Kostromskaja stanitza, and some graves near the Ulskaja stanitza;

(3) some graves in Northern Crimea (sixth to fifth centuries);[8]

(4) a group of graves on the middle Dnieper, of which the richest

is the barrow near the farm of Shumeiko (late sixth or early fifth century), and

(5) a grave discovered by the general Melgunov in the eighteenth century between the Dnieper and the Bug, of which the inventory is almost identical with the inventory of the Kelermes graves.

I have dealt at length with these graves in my two recent books, and need not repeat here what I have already said in them. The main characteristic features of the inventory of these graves might be summarized as follows. Many of the articles which were found in the graves were imported from abroad : some from Aeolian and Ionian Asia Minor, some probably from Persia. The latter are good representatives of an art which is usually called Phoenician or late Assyrian, and which was the art of the Near East during the domination of Assyria, the new Babylon and Persia.[9] There is, however, a special and large group of articles which show either an entirely different ornamental style or a mixture of motives, of which a part only is taken from the repertory of the so-called Phœnician or neo-Assyrian art, the rest being quite peculiar and original. The articles which are decorated in this manner are those which are peculiar to the Scythian life : their arms and weapons, their standards, the adornments of their horses. The workmanship of these articles is just the same as that which prevailed in the so-called Phœnician art, but the forms of the articles and the ornamental style are peculiar and original, and have nothing to do with the floral and animal style of the " Phoenician " art. It is evident that the articles were made on special order for the Scythian kings and princes by men who were trained in the " Phoenician " school of art, but who knew the customs, habits and ideas of the Scythians and were familiar also with the ornamental style which was probably the national style of the Scythians.

Let me briefly describe some of the articles which give the best idea of the Scythian style and which I reproduce on plates.

1. The most representative article, decorated partly in the " Phoeni-cian, " partly in the Scythian ornamental style, is the iron battle-axe of Kelermes, the handle and one part of the axe being covered with gold sheets adorned with figures in repoussé work with retouches made by chisel (PL. III and IV). The lower extremity of the handle and the hammer-end of the axe are adorned with antithetic groups of animals familiar to neo-Assyrian art and with common ornaments. Quite different is the ornamentation of the handle. The handle is covered from top to bottom by a sequence of crouched, standing or running animals, mostly various cervoids : antelopes, stags, reindeer and wild goats, but also wild boars and peculiar wild beasts, some similar to lions, some resembling bears. The rendering of the fur of all the animals by means of incised lines is one peculiarity of these figures; another is the peculiar treatment of the hoofs of the cervoids and the paws of the wild beasts; in two of the figures (PL. IV, 5; the second and fourth animal from below) the paws of a bear and the hoofs of a boar assume the form of eagle-heads; finally, the horns of the deer are treated in an original way with a pronounced tendency towards stylization.

2. A gold breast-plate of a man's armour or of a horse pectoral from Kelermes originally sewn on a leather backing (PL. V, 3). It is divided in twenty-four squares each filled with a figure of a crouched deer with ornamental horns. On the two long sides of the plate are two friezes of crouched lions.

3. A massive gold pectoral in the form of a half-crouched lion or lioness, from the same place (PL. V, 2). Each paw of the lion has the form of a curled lion, and the tail is covered with six figures of the same kind. The ears, the eyes and the nostrils of the animal are inlaid with amber, the ears in the technique of cloisonné work.[10]

4. A pair of standard tops from the Ulskaja stanitza (PL. VI, 1 and 2). Such standard tops are one of the peculiarities of the Scythian life

and burial ritual. They have mostly the shape of a big bell with the head of an animal on the top or the form of an animal head. In this present case, bells were hung up on the standard pole. Some of them belonged probably to the poles of a funeral canopy, some were used in the funeral procession as standards. The Ulskij pole-tops have the form of large eagle-heads, the beak being treated as a spiral and the eye as a human eye. Another eagle-head reduced to eye, beak and one ear, which shows that a griffon is meant, fills the free space between the beak and the eye of the big head. Four other smaller schematic eagle-heads form a frieze. The remaining space is covered with a figure of a crouched mountain-goat. Three bells were appended to each of the standard poles.

5. A pair of bronze " psalia " (parts of a horse-bridle fastened on both sides of the bit, and peculiar to Iranian bridles) from the same place (PL. VIII, 1). The upper parts of these psalia terminate in large eagle-heads. The free spaces on the heads are filled, on one of the psalia, by an engraved figure of a crouched hare, on the other by an engraved head of a rat or mouse. The rest of the upper parts of the psalia (body of the eagle ?) is covered by two partly engraved, partly sculptured figures of crouching lions, the shoulders of which are each adorned with an eagle's head ; behind the lions are engraved figures of a walking fox ( ?) and of a crouched ram ; the shoulder of the fox is adorned with an engraved eagle-head. The lower halves of the psalia represent crouched figures of eagle-griffons. Under the neck of the eagle-griffon is a reduced eagle-head (beak and eye). The paws of the lion body of the animal show the same form (beak and eye) and two beaks and eyes adorn the shoulder of the griffon. The remaining space (behind the tail of the griffon) is occupied by engraved figures of a crouched goat or deer and of a crouched bull. Similar psalia mostly of bone were found in large quantities in the archaic grave near the farm of Shumeiko (middle Dnieper). Some of them terminate in heads of mules, some are

covered with engraved abbreviations of an eagle's figure : beak, eye, wing (PL. VII, 5); some with engraved crouched figures of elks alternating with eagle-heads (PL. VII, 1, 2); some familiar eagle-head, the neck being inlaid in the technique of cloisonné (PL. VII, 3, 4, cf. 6). On one, the neck of an eagle-head is covered with an engraved figure of a curled lion with a curled nose, the centre of the body being occupied by a palmette (PL. VII, 7). It is worth noting that an almost exactly similar object has been found recently on the Volga in the government of Saratov (see text figure). It is also worth mentioning that a bronze eagle-head of the same type of stylization has been found in the earliest Scythian grave hitherto known, the grave on the Temirgora, along with a pendent in the form of a curled lion or griffon (PL. VI, 3, 4).

6. Finally I would like to describe two peculiar strap ends of bronze covered with gold in the form of a cross. One comes from the village Derevki (province of Kharkov; PL. VIII, 2). It consists of four circles forming a cross and of a rectangular end. The four circles are filled with figures of curled lions killing onagers. The square end is occupied by four figures of half-crouched lions. The other strap end was found in Olbia (PL. VIII, 3). It consists of three eagle-heads (reduced to beaks and eyes), a central medallion filled with the figure of a curled lion and a square end filled with two pairs of ram-heads. Almost identical strap ends adorned in the same style were found in Central Russia. This and other articles of the same style found in Central Russia show that the animal style came to Central Russia from South Russia.

There is not the slightest doubt that in the seventh and sixth centuries B.C. a new and peculiar animal style was brought into South Russia by the Scythian conquerors. The peculiarities of this style may be summarized as follows. (1) The tendency to give to a useful article the form of an animal or of a part of an animal, or to set on the top of the article an animal or a part of an animal; (2) adornment of an

article by figures or parts of animals ; (3) primitive arrangement of
these animals in rows or columns, almost no antithetic or synthetic
groups being used ; (4) tendency to fill up with these figures or parts
of them the whole available space — *horror vacui* — ; (5) naturalistic style in rendering the figures of the animals ; but (6) with a
tendency to transform some parts of them into ornaments (the horns
of deers) ; or (7) to treat them (especially the extremities) as animals
or as parts of animals (eagle-head, curled lions) ; (8) reduction of
the animals to their most typical parts : e.g. beak, eye and wing for
an eagle ; (9) predilection for real animals, fantastic animals being
an exception ; (10) peculiar choice of animals : various cervoids,
boars, reindeers, elks, eagles, a fauna of mountains and forests ; (11)
complete lack of human figures ; (12) no use of floral ornaments.

The second period in the evolution of the Scythian art in South
Russia is represented by some rich finds which must be dated in the
fifth and early fourth centuries B.C. The best known find of this
period is the Vettersfelde find in South East Prussia. To the same
group belong the earlier graves of a group of barrows on the Kuban,
which are called by the native population the " Seven Brothers ; "
some graves in the neighbourhood of the Greek city of Nymphaeum
in the Crimea (the largest part of the inventory now in the Ashmo-
lean Museum at Oxford), many articles of an unknown provenance
in the Berlin Museum and in the Metropolitan Museum of New York,
some graves on the middle Dnieper.

The group is characterized by : (1) an unusually large quantity
of articles imported from Persia (especially drinking horns of gold
and silver or with ornamental gold plaques) and from Ionian Greece
(especially pottery and bronzes), in the later part of this period Attic
imports being even more common, and (2) the fact that the typical
Scythian articles are no longer made by artists trained in the Asiatic
school, but by artists either trained by Ionians or themselves Ionians.
It is probable that the Greek cities of the Black Sea began to work

for the Scythians and that the Ionian artists either made in the Greek cities articles suitable to the taste of the Scythians, or were employed at the courts of Scythian kings and princes. The best evidence for this *rôle* of Ionian artists is presented by the find of Vettersfelde : typical Scythian articles adorned according to the principles of the Scythian animal style are treated stylistically in the purest Ionian fashion. The best evidence for the Persian import is presented by the *rhyta* (drinking horns) of the barrows of the " Seven Brothers. "

And yet the pure Scythian style has in no way faded away. While most of the articles in gold and silver were either imported or made by Ionian artists, the Scythian style displayed itself in the more modest parts of the grave furniture, especially in the small gold plaques which were sewn on the garments and the rugs and in the gold and bronze horse-trappings. Thousands of small plaques and hundreds of frontlets, bridle ornaments, psalia, etc. were found in the Scythian graves of the fifth century, and almost all of them follow the trend of evolution which had been devised by the earlier period. The Greek, especially the Ionian, influence is of course felt, but the style still remains an almost pure animal style, exhibiting all the peculiar features of the archaic art with some innovations and new creations in the same spirit.

Let me again reproduce and describe some of the most characteristic articles. The best sets were found in the barrows of the " Seven Brothers " and in the recently excavated barrows near the Elizavetinskaja stanitza on the Kuban.

1. A gold armour breast-plate in the form of a leaping stag with ornamental horns (PL. V, 1). This beautiful plaque was recently found in Hungary at Tapio-Szentmarton (see L. Bella in *Aréthuse*, 1925, IX, p. 140, f. and PL. XXVI). I owe to the kindness of Mr. L. Bella a photograph of this plaque. Similar plaques have been found repeatedly in South Russia in comparatively early Scythian graves (e.g. Kostromskaja stanitza, Kul-Oba, Smela, in chronological

order ; the plaque of the Kostromskaja stanitza belongs to the fifth century B.C., that of Kul-Oba to the early fourth century B.C., and that of Smela to the late fourth or early third century B.C.). The Hungarian plaque shows such a striking similarity to the Vettersfelde objects that I do not hesitate to assign to it an early date (late sixth, or early fifth century B.C.). It is well known that Hungary is very rich in Scythian graves of the early period.

2. A gold plaque from one of the tumuli of the "Seven Brothers" (PL. IX, 2). The plaque was originally nailed to the mouth of a drinking horn, of horn or wood. The fantastic beast represented on this plaque is a dragon with the head of a wolf (compare PL. II, 5, and PL. XI, 4), and paws of a lion ; the winged body (with typical oriental wings curled inward) ends in duck-head tail, after the Hittite manner. The head shows the volute-crest so typical for the griffons of the Orient and a strange horn-like beard. Note also the upturned nose ; there can be no doubt that the head is that of a wolf and not of a crocodile. The beast presents an odd mixture of Assyrian, Hittite and Scythian elements.

3. Another gold plaque from the same place and for the same use (PL. IX, 3). It is adorned with a symplegma of a lion killing a reindeer. While plaque No. 2 is certainly the product of a skilled artisan trained in the Ionian school, plaque No. 3 was no doubt done by a native workman. The combination of lion and reindeer reveals a better knowledge of the reindeer than of the lion.

4. A set of gold plaques now in the Metropolitan Museum (formerly in a private Russian collection ; PL. IX, 1). Beside some small geometric and floral plaques, there are some Iono-Persian figures of an eagle-griffon and some figures of reindeer with typical horns adorned with beaks and eyes of an eagle.

5. A set of bronze ornaments of horse-bridles and, perhaps, of chariots from the " Seven Brothers : " (a) head of an eagle with an Oriental

palmette at the back (PL. X, 4); (*b*) a bird of prey with a long beak, the beak being treated as a spiral, and with claws which terminate in spirals and remind one of the familiar beaks and eyes of the Scythian animal style (PL. X, 5); (*c*) a " psalion, " the figure of a lion in a twisted position, the upper part being turned left, the lower right (PL. X, 1); (*d*) naturalistic head of a " saiga " (steppe antelope : PL. X, 6); (*e*) a bridle or belt plaque, circular, filled with the figure of a curled lion (PL. X, 3); (*f*) a naturalistic boar's head (PL. X, 8); (*g*) figure of a crouched reindeer with the horns forming a palmette over its head (PL. X, 2); (*h*) head of an elk, the typical crest ending in a head of an eagle (PL. X, 7).

6. A set of bronze ornaments of horse-bridles from the barrows of the Elizavetinskaja stanitza : (*a*) a horned crouched dragon in a twisted position, the head and the forelegs turned upward, the body in the opposite natural direction, with open mouth, a set of sharp teeth and two large tusks, the lower jaw being treated as a spiral or an eagle-beak ; the head of the dragon is surmounted by deer horns treated ornamentally ; behind the horns is the typical crest ; the forelegs end in eagle-heads as also the tail and the hind legs (PL. XI, 2); (*b*) similar winged dragon in a natural position running to the right, the mouth wide open, the paws and the tail ending in eagle-heads (PL. XI, 1); (*c*) a psalion : the upper end formed like a couple of lions standing upright on their hind legs, the heads turned right and left correspondingly and their bodies in the opposite direction to the heads ; out of their mouths come two palmettes : openwork (PL. XI, 8); (*d*) a psalion : the lower end is formed like an elk's or reindeer's head turned right crowned with a rich palmette — a stylization of the horns : openwork (PL. XI, 9); (*e*) another psalion : two reindeers standing upright with heads turned right and left respectively and the bodies in the opposite direction to the heads, the horns forming a rich palmette or nimbus above the heads : openwork (PL. XI, 11); (*f*) a psalion : two dragons of the

same type as described above under (*a*) and (*b*), in the same heraldic position as in (*c*) and (*e*), below two heads of indistinct beasts biting into the bodies of the dragons ( ?) : openwork (PL. XI, 10) ; (*g*) a dragon's or wolf's head left, with open mouth, sharp teeth, two big tusks and upturned nose ending into a spiral : openwork (PL. XI, 4) ; (*h*) a psalion : the upper part consists of two lion's heads on long necks and an eagle-head on a shorter neck, all left (PL. XI, 7) ; (*i*) a psalion : the upper part represents a reindeer's horn, each branch of the horn ending in eagle's heads : openwork (PL. XI, 6) ; (*k*) a bridle plaque : reindeer right in a circle : openwork (PL. XI, 3) ; (*l*) a bridle plaque : three goat's heads forming a solar wheel : openwork (PL. XI, 5).

The general impression which is produced by the study of the horse implements of the fifth and early fourth centuries B.C. is that of the great progress made by the Scythian or half-Scythian artisans. They have learned a good deal from their Ionian colleagues. They adopted the antithetic or heraldic group. They introduced some of the plant ornaments. They took over the figures of some fantastic animals, especially the dragon, which reminded them of some of the animals of their forests. The figure of the dragon had an enormous success and spread far and wide over Central and Eastern Russia. And, last but not least, they tried to introduce some peculiar rhythm into their creations and thus to make the animal style a real ornamental style. It is, of course, a matter of taste. But to me the animal palmette formed out of horned animals is as important an artistic creation as the plant and flower palmette of the art of the Near East and of Greece. Whether the Scythian artisans imitated Greek palmettes or came to the palmette solution of their ornamental problem by themselves, is a question which we are not able to solve.

At any rate, the Scythian animal style in the hands of the Scythian artisans of the fifth century has lost a good deal of its primitiveness and savagery. It showed a serious endeavour to develop this animal style into a regular ornamental style, where the animal figure would play the same *rôle* as the plant and the flower played in Oriental and Greek decorative art. However, the art of the Scythians was confined to a minor and subsidiary *rôle*. The Scythians never built temples, palaces or cities. They were nomads and lived in tents. How far the principles of the animal style were used in the architecture and adornment of these tents we do not know. The carpets for example were a splendid field for a display of animal motives, but the few textiles which were found in Scythian graves are imports from Ionian Greece. Some fragments recently found in Mongolia show that, at least in later times, the animal style in its later form was used in the textile industry of Central Asia, but no evidence exists for the earlier period and for South Russia. The wood used for the tents has completely disappeared, and there was not very much of it in the visible parts of a tent. Stone architecture remained unknown and was not used by the Scythians. And even the larger and more costly pieces of furniture were not made by native artisans, but bought from and made by the Ionian. The taste of the Scythian chiefs became more and more Hellenized, and they tolerated the Scythian animal style rather than promoted and encouraged it. Thus the Scythian animal style, confined to articles of minor importance, was bound gradually to decay, and this is what happened in the next period.

To this period — the later fourth century — belong the most imposing and the richest barrow-graves of South Russia. Scores of them were found all over the Scythian steppes : Kul-Oba near Panticapaeum, Karagodeuashch in the East, the splendid set of graves to the East and to the West of the lower Dnieper : Chertomlyk, Solokha, the group of Serogozy, etc., the group on the middle Dnieper near Smela and near Romny, scattered graves farther to the West (e.g. Ryzanovka), an interesting group on the middle Don, and some graves in Bulgaria, Hungary and Rumania,[11] all belong to this chronological group, as well as hundreds of minor graves. I have demonstrated elsewhere that the beginning of the political decay of the Scythian Empire was its period of greatest development as regards material welfare.

The art of this period is well known to us. The most interesting feature of it is the fact that along with imports, especially from Athens (e.g. pottery), the best articles in the graves were certainly made in South Russia for the Scythian rulers. The artist who worked in the Ionian κοινή (common Ionian artistic style), be he a man who lived in Olbia or at the Scythian courts, disappeared and was replaced by an artist who followed his own path and who had his own style. This style apparently was created at Panticapaeum and adapted itself to the peculiar conditions by which it had been created. The Panticapaean artists were working not for Greeks, but for Scythians, and had to suit their taste. Most of them were toreutic craftsmen and jewellers. They had to learn, just as their Ionian predecessors, the forms of the articles which were in common use in Scythia. And in order to be successful, they had to follow the change in the ideas and in the taste of their customers. The customers no longer asked for a purely ornamental decoration of their articles in the Ionian animal style. They became more ambitious. They wanted their life — military and religious — portrayed on their sacred vessels, on their arms and on their garments. The artists understood it, and we owe to this peculiar phenomenon the delightful set of articles on which the Scythian life is depicted with understanding and sympathy in realistic and romantic scenes. Along with these, there still survived the articles decorated in the Ionian animal style. But it was now the new Ionian style, as it existed in Asia Minor in the fourth century B.C. Finally, as in Etruria, some Greek mythological scenes were added to the Scythian repertoire which they probably interpreted in their own way.

The Scythian animal style did not disappear. Confined as it was to minor articles (especially horse-trappings) and used by common artisans, it certainly degenerated. The Russian museums are full of such bronze articles, mostly constituent parts of horse-trappings. Life has gone out of them. What the artisans who made them did was to repeat old motives over and over again. No new motives are noticeable, no new artistic ideas. The craft was in full stagnation and gradually decayed. I abstain from reproducing and describing any articles of this degenerated style (one of the bell-standards of this or a little earlier period is represented on PL. XII, 4). There are thousands of them and all repeat the same motives, often so disfigured as to make them a real puzzle for those who have not studied the style in its evolution. Concerning the new elements of decoration and the new articles which appear in these Scythian graves of the last period, I shall speak in the next chapter [12].

# NOTES

## CHAPTER I

1. On the " Tripolje " civilization or the civilization of the " Agriculturalists of the Black-Earth Region " see V. Gordon Childe, *The Dawn of European Civilization*, 1925, p. 152 ff. The question of this civilization is far from being solved and cannot be solved without the publication of all the material which is stored in the Russian Museums and without new extended excavations. Meanwhile a general monograph on the South Russian finds, which has been prepared by Th. Volkov, but never published, is highly desirable. Comp. the summary of an article of B. L. Bogayevsky in *Amer. Journ. Arch.* 30 (1926), p. 350 f. In this note Bogayevsky speaks of the recent finds and excavations in Russia and Poland (since 1916) which bear on the problem of the Tripolje civilization. A useful map showing the location of the new excavated places, and a short bibliography of the most recent works are incorporated in the note. Cf. the various articles, especially those of V. Kozlovska, P. Kourinny, N. Makarenko in *La Culture de Tripolié en Ukraine*, VOL. I, Kiev, 1926 (in Russian, published by the Academy of Science of the Ukraine), and V. Danilevic, *The Archaeological Past of the Region of Kiev*, Kiev, 1925 (in Russian).

2. On the Kuban finds or the civilization of the *People of the Steppes* — V. Gordon Childe, l.c., p. 138 ff. The problem whether the " bearers of battle axes, " " the battle axe people " moved from north to south, or from southeast to northwest is hotly debated. The last word has not yet been said. We must await new and more systematic excavations in the Northern and Central Caucasus and the publication of the treasures of the Museum of Tiflis which certainly will throw more light on the material found in the " ochre " graves of the steppes of South Russia. Like the " agriculturalists of the black-earth region " the " battle axe people " left almost no traces in the later life of the South Russian steppes.

3. A. M. Tallgren has dealt with the group of the Kuban finds repeatedly. His earlier works on this subject are quoted by V. Gordon Childe (see *Note* 2). In his two recent articles on the subject (*Fatjanovokulturen i Centralryssland* in *Sartryk ur Finskt Museum*, 1924, and *Zur frühenv. Metallkultur Sudrusslands* in *Studien zur vorgeschichtlichen Archaeologie Alfred Goetze dargebracht*, hrsg. von H. Motefindt, Leipzig, 1925, p. 66 ff; cf. his article *Fatjanovo-Kultur* in *Reallexikon der Vorgeschichte*) he is inclined to date the Kuban civilization in the beginning of the second millenium (B.C. 1700-1500). Compare his treatment of this question in the light of new evidence, in his recent book *La Pontide préscythique*, 1926, p. 82 ff. and *passim*. His date is based on comparisons of articles of the graves with those common to certain periods of the Minoan civilization. I must confess that his parallels have not convinced me. It was Tallgren who first pointed out how great was the influence of the Kuban region on Central Russia (the so-called Fatjanovo civilization).

4. On the civilization of the so-called ochre graves and on the bronze period in South Russia in general see the recent book of A. M. Tallgren, *La Pontide préscythique* ( in *Eurasia Septentrionalis Antiqua*, 2, 1926), where the material has been collected and organized for

the first time. The Koban articles found in South Russia are enumerated by Tallgren in the book quoted above, on p. 222. On the finds of Mihalkovo, etc. and on the Kuban civilization see my Introduction, *Note* 11.

5. I have collected the evidence on the Scythians and have retold their history in my recent book : *Iranians and Greeks in South Russia*, 1922.

6. The most recent contribution to the very vexed question on the origin of the Scythians, as far as this origin is revealed by the scanty remains of their language, is that of M. Vasmer *Untersuchungen über die altesten Wohnsitze der Slaven*, VOL. I, *Die Iranier in Südrussland*, 1923. Vasmer collected in this little book all the words and names which are connected with the Scythians and analyzed them carefully. He comes to the conclusion that so far as our linguistic evidence goes we must assume that the Scythians belonged to the Iranian stock.

7. I summarize here, with some slight modifications, my detailed studies on this subject of which I gave another longer summary in my book quoted in *Note* 5 of this chapter. The full evidence on which my division is based is incorporated in my book : *Scythia and the Bosporus*, St. Petersburg, 1925. In my English book and especially in the Russian volume I gave a detailed description and a full bibliography of all the most important graves and chance finds of the Scythian and Sarmatian period in South Russia. Reproductions of the most important articles which were found in the Scythian and Sarmatian graves may be easily found either in Kondakoff-Tolstoi-Reinach, *Antiquités de la Russie Méridionale*, or in E. H. Minns, *Scythians and Greeks*, 1913, or in my English book. The illustrations in M. Ebert, *Südrussland im Altertum*, 1920, are far from satisfactory.

8. See the recent treatment of the Scytho-Sarmatian graves of the Crimea by A. Spizyn in *Scytho-Sarmatian Barrows of the Crimean Steppes*, in the *Bulletin of the Taurian Archaeological Commission*, 54, 1918, p. 1 ff. (in Russian).

9. The last treatment of this school of art has been recently given by F. von Bissing in *Jahrb. d. d. Arch. Inst.*, 38-39, 1924, p. 180 ff.

10. I cannot treat here the question of the polychromy of the early Scythian art. I must note, however that this polychromy is shortlived in South Russia. It appears in the archaic period and later disappears completely. In the later products of the Perso-Ionian art and especially in the Panticapaean jewels of the fourth century B.C. a soft and delicate polychromy of the Persian type (a kind of enamel coupled with granulate work) reappears again but is used with great moderation. The origin of the early polychromy in the Scythian art is still a problem. Strzygowski is inclined to look for its origin to Central Asia. I came to the same conclusion independently. However, the arguments of O. M. Dalton (*East Christian Art*, 1925, p. 321 and in the *Antiquaries Journal*, VOL. IV, 1924, p. 261), who advocates the Egyptian origin of the cloisonné technique, are very strong and cannot be disregarded. I must add that along with Egypt, Sumer and Babylonia excelled in this technique from the earliest times (see my article *Sarmatian and Indo-Scythian Antiquities* in *Recueil d'études dédiées à la mémoire de N. P. Kondakoff*, 1926, p. 240, *Note* 1) and that, as Dalton has pointed out (*Archæologia*, 58, 1903, p. 237 ff.), this tradition was kept and developed by the artistic χοινή of the first millenium B.C. The technique of the early Scythian finds

is not different if compared with that of the famous ivory figurines of Nimrûd and it is not improbable that the Scythian artists borrowed it from the Near East. Another possible solution is that the *cloisonné* polychromy came in a very early period from Central Asia both to Sumer and Egypt and that later it was imported to South Russia by the Scythians. I do not think however, that this solution is the most probable.

11. On the Bulgarian finds see my article : *Sarmatian and Indo-Scythian Antiquities* in *Recueil N. P. Kondakoff*, 1926, p. 243. On the finds of Roumania and Hungary, V. Parvan, *Getica*, p. 3 ff., 728 ff., PLS. I, VII. The late V. Parvan, whose premature death deprived Roumania of her leading archaeological and historical force, was the first to collect and to illustrate the Scytho-Sarmatian antiquities of Roumania. Some of the objects collected by him shown on PLS. I, VII, are, however, of a much later date and not Scytho-Sarmatian. Cf. G. I. Bratianu, *Le Poignard scythe de Boureni* (Moldavie) in *Dacia*, 1925, VOL. II, p. 417 ff.

12. The gradual degeneration of some of the motives of the animal style in this period is shown in the article of K. Malkina in *Jahrb. d. D. Arch. Inst.*, 1926, p. 176 ff.

# CHAPTER II

## THE ANIMAL STYLE IN SOUTH RUSSIA
## THE SARMATIAN PERIOD

J UST at the time when our historical written sources speak of the downfall of the Scythian Empire and the gradual advance of the Sarmatians, we notice in the civilization and in the art of South Russia, as revealed by the many finds in the graves of this period, a conspicuous change. In the latest Scythian graves, those of the late fourth and early third centuries B.C., especially in the graves of the big barrow of Alexandropole (in the lower Dnieper region), in some graves on the middle Don (Mastjughino) and in some graves of the middle Dnieper, the funeral constructions and the burial ritual remain unchanged. However, in the inventory, along with the usual imports from Greece, with the articles of the Panticapæan artists (and their imitations by Scythian artisans) and with the Scythian little gold plaques and horse-trappings, new articles hitherto unknown appear in ever larger quantities: articles which have no precedents in the Scythian graves.

Side by side with the usual Scythian horse-trappings we notice a new fashion of adorning the horses coming in. Along with the usual frontlets, cheek-pieces, strap-plaques and psalia of solid gold or bronze, done mostly in a plastic, but more often in an openwork technique reproducing whole figures or parts of animals, there appear gold or silver convex plaques of circular or oval shape with ornaments in repoussé. These become the most common adornments of the bridle, of the breast and of the croup-straps. The style of these plaques is not the Scythian animal style. The figures of animals, the various ornaments, etc. of these plaques have nothing in common with the well known types which were extensively used by the Scythian artisans. The nearest parallels to the new style which prevails on the plaques may be found in the late Achaemenid finds of the Oxus

and of Susa and in the contemporary Irano-Indian art of Çandragupta
and Açoka. And the habit itself of adorning the bridles with circular
plaques is Assyrian and Iranian or rather Iranian and Assyrian, not
Scythian. From the Persians this habit was taken over by the Greeks.
The best examples of these peculiar circular plaques are those from
the Alexandropole barrow, those from the Bobritzkoi grave-field
(middle Dnieper) and those from Panaguristshe in Bulgaria. To the
same group belongs a grave on the Taman peninsula (Vasjurinskaja
Gora).

Along with the new horse-trappings, some articles of an equally
new form made their appearance in the well established traditional set
of metal ornaments which were used by the Scythians as constituent
parts of their dress. The most conspicuous new article was a new form
of belt clasp, the hook-clasp (PL. XII, 1, 2). This clasp is completely
foreign to the Scythian dress of the early period, but is common both
in Central Asia and Central Russia and in China in the Hellenistic
period. It is worthy of note that this clasp of a new form is adorned
with motives taken from the repertory of the Scythian animal style.
A very curious coincidence of which I am speaking more fully
in the *Note* is the fact that exactly the same form of a hook-clasp
appears at the same time in Italy (PL. XII, 3).[1]

There is no doubt that these new articles were brought into the
Scythian life and art by the infiltration into the Scythian aristocracy
of some new groups of men, probably of the same ethnical origin,
but with a different civilization : a civilization which was closely akin
to the late Persian civilization. These new-comers were certainly the
first Sarmatians, whose Iranian origin is proved by the scanty remains
of their language.

A little later — in the third century B.C. — a new type of jewellery
began to replace the now old-fashioned Ionian and Attic jewellery
(or imitation of it by Scythian artists), in the Scythian graves. This
jewellery of which the most marked feature is the extensive use of

polychromy, effected by insets of precious and semi-precious stones either in the cloisonné or in the champlevé technique, is also of Persian origin. We know this jewellery from the late Achaemenid examples in the Oxus treasure and in the famous late Achaemenid grave of Susa. Not only a new style is in evidence, but new forms of jewellery are introduced as well. The most interesting new type is the circular brooch inset with jewels, which is so familiar to the students of Merovingian antiquities.

The new jewellery is found in many graves of South Russia of the third century B.C. The best dated and the richest are those of the Taman peninsula and of Gorgippia (modern Anapa). The most ancient circular brooch which we know was found in one of the graves of the Zelenskaja group of barrows (Taman peninsula) and is dated by coins and Greek articles in the late fourth or early third century B.C. It is important to note that along with this new type of jewellery many imported Persian articles appear again in the graves of the third and following centuries B.C., just as they had in the fifth century B.C. The most interesting examples are some graves in the region of the Ural river (Orenburg) full of late Achaemenid imports, graves which find their exact parallel in one of the graves of the Taman peninsula, the so-called Buerova Mogila. [2]

Still later, in the second century B.C., as we know from our literary sources, the Sarmatians appeared in South Russia in compact masses, one tribe after another, and occupied the steppes of South Russia first, from the Ural to the Dnieper, and later to the Danube. Their advance is marked by the almost complete disappearance of Scythian graves, and by the gradual spread of new forms of burial similar to, but in no way identical with the Scythian ones. I have described these forms of burial elsewhere. Here I must concentrate my attention on the art which has been revealed in these burials. Some of the most peculiar features of this art appear on the new type of horse-trappings of this period. The Scythian horse-trappings vanished almost completely. They were replaced by a completely new set of metal articles, the most prominent being bronze or iron rings instead of psalia, and circular silver-gilt " phalerae " of a semi-globular shape, as bridle, breast and croup-strip ornaments, instead of the Scythian openwork figures of animals, combinations of animals or parts of animals. These " phalerae " are decorated by figures of gods and animals in high and low relief, and by some plant and floral ornaments of the same technique and of a peculiar style.

I have devoted a special article to the analysis of this new style of decoration. The only parallels with these and other similar South Russian articles which I know are to be found exclusively in Iranized and Hellenized Northern India of the time of the Indo-Scythian and Parthian domination. The finds of South Russia and Bulgaria which best represent the new style — those of the Severskaja stanitza in the Kuban region, of Taganrog on the Don, of Starobelsk near Kharkov, of Yanchokrak near Melitopol, of Galiche in Bulgaria, and of the kingdom of Pontus — are all dated in the end of the second and the first centuries B.C. To the same time belong many similar articles, which are quite common in the Gandhara region, at Taxila and in the Pundjab in Northern India on one side and in all of Parthia on the other. [3]

Parallel to this peculiar development of toreutics, the jewellery of the second and first centuries B.C. was moving on the path which had been devised by the preceding period. Polychromy became all dominant. The symphony of colours, not the symphony of animal or plant forms, is now the final goal of those artists and artisans who supply the jewels for the graves of the Kuban region and of the steppes of South Russia of the late Hellenistic period. I have dealt with this jewellery in many of my books and articles. I have shown its beginnings, its development in South Russia and its migration to Western Europe in the third and the following centuries A.D. [4]

It is obvious that this new style of jewellery came to South Russia with the Sarmatians, and there is no doubt that the place whence it was brought into South Russia was the same which created and adopted the peculiar new fashion of horse-trappings described above. This region, undoubtedly, is the former Bactrian kingdom and Parthia, where the Persian jewellery was always the leading fashion. This is shown by a comparison of the jewellery found in South Russia, especially the jewellery of the burial grounds of Bori and Usahelo in the Caucasus, and that of the Kuban region, with the jewellery found at Taxila during the recent excavations of this opulent and large city by Sir John Marshall. [5]

Evidently, the new waves of Sarmatians, like those which had reached South Russia in the third century B.C., came from the confines of the Bactrian kingdom, the former provinces of the Persian Empire. In the second century B.C. these lands were the theatre of important though little known events. The former neighbours of China — the Yue-chi — whether Iranian or Turks (who, however, shared the Iranian civilization) were forced by the pressure of the Huns to leave their residence on the western frontier of the Chinese Empire and to move westward toward the rich regions occupied by the former subjects of the Persian Empire — the Sakians, who inhabited the plains near the Aral Sea and between the Aral and the Caspian Seas. These Sakians (the Greek sources call them Massagetai and Dahi) — already disturbed by the conquest of Alexander, by the successes of the early Seleucids and later by the early Bactrian and Parthian kings, and of whom one part had migrated to the confines of the crumbling Scythian Empire — were now pushed from the North and the East to the South and to the West. One part of them occupied a portion of the former Bactrian kingdom ; another settled in India, on the lower course of the Indus, after a hard fight with the Parthians. Many tribes apparently moved on the trail of their former neighbours and kinsmen beyond the Caspian Sea toward the South Russian plains. Having crossed the Ural and the Volga, they appeared, one tribe after another, in South Russia, and occupied the Kuban region. They then crossed the Don, the Dnieper, the Bug, and made their first appearance in the Balkan peninsula, pushing before them those tribes of the Sakians who had settled in Russia in the fourth and third centuries. The Greeks gave them the general name of Sarmatians or Sauromatians, which originally belonged probably to some tribes of the Mæotians, i.e. of the population which lived near the Sea of Asov. [6]

The art which these new-comers brought with them was not their own. They borrowed it from their neighbours and former masters. It was Persian in its main essence. The motives of the Scythian animal style are few and exceptional in this neo-Persian art, and those which were borrowed from the Scythians gradually decayed and disappeared. However, behind the Sakians moved the Yue-chi. It is well known how, about the first century A.D., they conquered the Indo-Scythian states and those Greco-Indian states which still lingered in India, and how they established themselves under a Kushan dynasty in India, as powerful neighbours of the Parthians. It is very probable that, arrested in their progress westwards by the Parthians in the South, they spread far and wide into South Siberia, and finally reached through Turkestan the steppes of South Russia. [7]

Their appearance or their pressure on their new neighbours is marked, both in Asia and in South Russia, by a new period in the development of art. Along with the type of art which I have previously described and which is represented by many finds, we have some finds which show common features with those mentioned above, but along with these features some very important peculiarities. The artists who made the articles of which these finds consist adopted the polychrome tendency, but at the same time they stressed their inclination towards the extensive use of the motives of a new animal style, which is certainly a branch of the Scythian animal style, but shows many new peculiarities foreign to the Scythians.

The most important finds of this new type are : (1) a chance discovery near Maïkop in the Kuban region, which is closely related to another chance discovery made supposedly in Bulgaria ; (2) a find made in the territory of the city of Novocherkassk and some other related minor finds in the steppes of South Russia, especially on the Don ; and (3) the set of gold plaques and jewels found in the eighteenth century in Siberia (the exact site of the discovery is unknown), the largest part of which is in the Hermitage, though another part came into the possession of Witsen in Holland and has apparently been lost after its publication by Witsen.

1. The finds of Maïkop and of Bulgaria :

(a) The Maïkop belt (PL. XIII, 1, 2). How and when this belt was discovered is unknown. It is now in the Hermitage. The belt is complete. It consists of a hook-clasp and of a series of links connected with each other by the leather strip of the belt. The material is silver or silver-plated bronze. The clasp (a hook-clasp) is formed by two animals (a griffon and a horse). A fierce winged eagle-griffon is on the left (turned right), its back turned to the spectator, its wings curled in the oriental fashion. The claws of its lion's body are disproportionately large. The head, which forms the hook of the clasp, is plunged into the neck of the horse on the right (turned left). The figure of the griffon is full of ferocious energy and very expressive. The ferocity of the attack is expressed in all the muscles of the body, especially in the head and the back. At the lower end of the right wing a cornelian is fitted into a circular setting. The horse is represented in death-agony with its head well down, the mouth half open, the eyes half closed. The agony is expressed also in the neck and in the forelegs. The figure is full of pathos, as impressive as the best figures of the dying animals in Assyrian art. The hind legs of the horse are twisted and the croup is turned to the spectator, like the croup of the griffon and for the same purpose, i.e. for inserting into the bodies of the two animals the first links of the belt. The ear of the horse was filled by a cornelian. The same insertions were used at the joints of the horse, where triangular cornelians are set into special settings, in a technique which is almost identical with that used for the lioness of the Kelermes find described above. The pair of animals are fighting in a forest which is indicated by two stylized trees. The links of the belt represent, each of them, a stylized figure of a flying eagle seen from below. The heads of the eagles are transformed into a geometric ornament, a set of semi-circular and triangular settings filled with cornelians. On the back, where the last two links of the belt meet, a big square cornelian is inset. The belt as a whole is one of the greatest achievements of the animal style coupled with the polychrome style.

(*b*) Another belt of the same type has been found, as is alleged, in Bulgaria and is now in the British Museum (PL. XIII, 3). The belt clasp consists of four animals. The hook is formed by a figure of an eagle seen from the front. The eagle holds in its claws a sheep. The belt hole is formed by two animals — a boar, right, biting into the neck of the eagle, and behind the boar a deer in the usual crouched position. The horns of the deer are stylized and form a kind of a scroll which fills the space between the boar and the upper frame of the belt. Another plant scroll begins under the neck of the deer and fills the space between the back of the boar and the first link of the belt. The ear of the boar forms a triangle in which a cornelian is inset. The links of the belt are formed by two eagle-heads facing each other and between them a geometrized figure of an eagle, with spread wings consisting of five settings filled with cornelians. With the belt were found ornamental plaques in the form of a solar wheel (see the first vignette). In the centre of a circle : — three concentric circles and a geometric rosette inset with cornelians ; four eagle-griffon or dragon heads form the wheel, all looking left ; the lips of the dragons are treated as spirals ; on the cheeks, a floral rosette in the technique of champlevé.

2. A rich find of articles of the same type as those described under No. 1 was made in 1864 in a barrow-grave called Khokhlach near the city of Novocherkassk (Don). The find is in the Hermitage. It has been published and described many times, so that it is unnecessary to repeat the descriptions. Let me make some short remarks on the most conspicuous articles of the find :

(a) The diadem (see Rostovtzeff, *Iranians and Greeks*, PL. XXVI, 1). It is an interesting mixture of Greek forms (the form of the diadem is Greek) and ornaments (the beautiful Hellenistic cameo, the pendents, the figures of the owl), of a rich polychromy of inset stones, as well as of the motives of a savage animal style (reindeer and goats in a forest). The combination is unique and the object certainly was produced by a native artist under a strong Greek influence.

(b) The openwork gold torque (PL. XIV, 1). It consists of two sets of eagle-griffons turned left in the lower register and right in the upper, separated by three concentric gold circles. The joints of the bodies of the griffons have inset stones in the champlevé technique.

(c) Two gold armlets of four spirals each (PL. XIV, 4, 5). The ends of the armlets consist of two sets of crouched dragons with upturned noses formed as spirals. On the joints — inset cornelians.

(d) Three little boxes with lids and one bottle suspended on a chain also with a lid, all of gold (Rostovtzeff, *Iranians and Greeks*, PL. XXVI, 3). The bodies of these articles are covered with a symphony of animals in synthetic groups : a reindeer (female) attacked and killed by a tiger and an eagle. On the lids of the boxes — three female reindeer. The same animals in a row on the neck of the bottle. The lid of the bottle is filled with the figure of a curled reindeer or elk. All the figures are inset with stones.

(e) A gold cup (Minns, *Scythians and Greeks*, p. 235, *fig.* 144). The handle reproduces a figure of a standing reindeer (inset stones). A similar cup was found at the Migulinskaja stanitza (I. Smirnoff,

*Argenterie Orientale*, PL. X, 27). It bears an inscription which gives the names of the owner (Xebanokos) and of the artist (Tarulas). The first name is probably Sarmatian, the second Thracian.

(*f*) A scent bottle (Rostovtzeff, l.c., PL. XXVI, 2). The body consists of a hollow cylinder of agate; the extremities are of gold and reproduce the forepart and the hindpart of the body of a lion.

(*g*) The most remarkable piece of the find (PL. XIV, 2, 3). It is an étui-case of gold, with inset turquoise and with a gold chain attached to its ends. The body of the case is covered with three figures of tigers biting each others' bodies. The beasts are almost identical with the well known hydrae of Chinese art. The same elongated body, the same agility, the same ferocity. One of the hydrae has enveloped a dying horse in the coils of its body. I shall come back to this remarkable objet, but shall not describe all the remaining various articles of the find, since the set which I have described is sufficient for my purpose.

I may add that articles of the type of those of Novocherkassk were found all over the Northern Caucasus and South Russia, but not in large quantities, nor predominating. Predominant in these places is the polychrome style, the stones being connected by and framed in geometric ornaments. However, from time to time traces of the neo-animal style are found in graves where the geometric polychrome style predominates. One of the most interesting articles is the gold plaque from the Kuban, with the figure of a winged wolf-dragon in a setting of stylized leaves (symbolizing a forest) and with inset stones all over the body (Kondakoff, Tolstoi, Reinach, *Antiquités de la Russie Méridionale*, PL. 486, *fig.* 440; Minns, l.c., PL. 279, *fig.* 205). Armlets and torques in the same animal style are quite common, especially in the Eastern part of the steppes of South Russia.

3. The various gold articles found in Siberia in the eighteenth century,

now in the Hermitage. The circumstances under which these articles were excavated are unknown, and equally unknown is the place where the find was made. The uniformity of the style in most of the articles and the fact that our evidence points to Western Siberia show that probably most of the articles were excavated in one place and belong to the same time. Whether it was one rich grave which was excavated or a series of such graves, we are unable to tell. All the articles of the find have never been published and carefully illustrated. A catalogue was prepared by the late G. Kieseritzky, but his manuscript is not published. I cannot describe all the articles in this book, since this can be done only by one who has daily access to the treasures of the Hermitage. I must however reproduce and describe some of them, those of which I happen to have good photographs. The whole set might be subdivided in two large sections : (*a*) heavy gold plaques in openwork technique partly with inset stones ;[8] and (*b*) a set of heavy gold jewels : torques, armlets, mirrors, rings, ear-rings, etc.

One piece must be described separately. It is the famous armlet with the ends formed as figures of crouched lion-griffons (Minns, l.c.). The bodies of these griffons are adorned with a profusion of coloured stones. On the neck these stones form a solid field subdivided by gold cloisons. The technique is Persian, and it was evident to all those who have dealt with this article that it had been produced in the same workshops where some of the articles of the Oxus treasure were made. It is equally evident that articles like this were the originals of those of local workmanship which appear in the majority of the Siberian find or finds.

(A) 1. Most prominent among the heavy gold plaques of Siberia is the famous gold eagle which might have served as a crest (Minns, l.c., p. 273, *fig.* 192). The eagle (which has not a reptile head, as Minns says, but the head of an eagle-griffon) is represented with wide spread wings and an erect tail. It holds an ibex in its claws. Red stones were inset in the cloisons of the breast and of the lower part of the wings. The tail might have been adorned with real feathers. There is a striking similarity between this eagle and the eagle of the belt from Bulgaria, and still more striking is the similarity between the ibex of the Siberian plaque and the horse of the Maïkop belt. We find the same twisted position of the body, the hind legs being turned in the opposite direction to the body and head. Again the same attempt at rendering the unconquerable energy of the eagle and the miserable agony of the ibex.

2. Almost a repetition of the clasp of the Maïkop belt is the group of the lion-griffon killing a horse (PL. XV, 1). There is the same ferocious energy and the same pathos. But one sees that it is only a repetition, while the Maïkop belt is the original work of a great artist.

3. The same spirit permeates the group of an eagle killing a yak, while a tiger sitting on its hind-legs is ferociously biting the eagle's tail (PL. XV, 2, 3). The eagle has ears, and therefore is an eagle-griffon. Excellent workmanship. The beasts are full of pathos, the composition is faultless. Along with the Maïkop belt, it is the best production of the neo-animal style.

4. A very interesting group is that of a dragon engaged in a fierce fight with a tiger (PL. XVI, 1). The dragon has the typical upturned nose and a crest which consists of four eagle-griffon heads. The same kind of head forms the extremity of its tail.

5. More peaceful is the fight between a fantastic being (with an eagle-griffon's head, with reindeer's horns ending in eagle-griffon's heads and with a similarly constructed tail) and a small tiger (PL. XVII, 1). The forepart of the big animal is adorned with a figure of an eagle-griffon, the hindpart with the head of a yak. This head is devoured by a large eagle-griffon head,

which at the same time forms the tail of the eagle-griffon described above. A similar head forms the end of the tail of the animal.

6. Quite schematic is the group of a big beast (tiger) devouring a small camel (PL. XVII, 2). Behind the group, a tree.

7. An attempt to portray life in the forest is made in two plaques of the set. In one (PL. XVI, 2) a mountain forest is represented (the stones of a mountainous ground are indicated by a set of inset stones in the right corner). Climbing the mountain is a dog, which is scared and barks at the scene taking place in the forest. Two horsemen are hunting a boar. One runs at full gallop in the woods, shooting an arrow from his bow at a boar in full flight. His dress, his sword, his long-haired head and moustaches remind one of the pictures of Sarmatians in the Panticapæan art and of the portraits of the Kushan kings in India. Note also the tassels behind the saddle, which reappear later on Sassanian and Chinese monuments. The sword is exactly the same which was later borrowed by the Goths from the Sarmatians, and very similar to the swords lately discovered in Korea in Chinese graves of the period.[9] The other hunter has dismounted. He holds his frightened horse (note the circular plaques of its trappings) by the bridle; although he has climbed a tree to save his life. He tries to make the horse climb the tree which has saved his own life. He looks at the running boar which is attacking his horse.[10] Another similar plaque shows a less vivid scene : a man resting under a tree on the knees of his wife, while a servant is holding two saddled horses. A quiver is hanging on the tree (Minns, l.c.).

(B) 1. A gold openwork armlet formed by three rings, each of which shows a symphony of wild beasts (griffons, dragons, etc.), killing other animals. The bodies are shown in various equally unnatural positions (PL. XVIII, 2).

2. A similar armlet (PL. XVIII, 3).

3. A torque which ends in the figure of a lion (Minns, l.c., p. 272, *fig.* 191).

4. A torque ending in a figure of a dragon. The crest is formed by eight eagle-griffon's heads, and the double tail ends in a pair of similar heads (PL. XVIII, 1).

5. The same figure adorns a plaque which was fastened to a belt (?) (PL. XVIII, 4).

6. A lid of a toilet box showing a fight between an eagle-griffon with reindeer's horns, and a tiger (PL. XVII, 4).

7. An openwork mirror adorned with a series of aquatic birds (PL. XVII, 3).

Similar articles are exhibited in some of our museums, and certainly come from Siberia. Such are, e.g. the two gold plaques in the Metropolitan Museum : one showing a heraldic group of two tigers killing two ibexes (PL. XXVIII, 2); another an eagle-griffon holding in its claws a sheep (Rostovtzeff, *Aréthuse*, 1927, PL. XV, 5 ; cf. XVI, 1).

Before characterizing the new stage in the evolution of the animal style which is represented by the articles described above, I must say a few words on the date of the three groups which I have described. No one of them can be dated with the same certainty as was possible for the Scythian groups. No pottery, no coins were found with the articles. The Roman and Chinese coins supposed to have been found with the Siberian things might have been found elsewhere. There is no certainty. We must therefore rely upon a stylistic analysis.

The earliest articles are the two belts described under No. 1. The belt of Bulgaria, especially in the figures of the boar and that of the deer, is so strikingly similar to some of the figures of the late Scythian animal style, especially those of the barrow of Alexandropole, that we have no right to separate sharply one from the other. And yet both the Bulgarian and the Maïkop belts breathe a different spirit, which is evident if they are compared with the decaying Scythian animal style of the third century B.C. The artist of the Maïkop belt lived probably in an area where he still met some residua of the dying Scythian style. The late second century B.C. would not be too early a date for both belts, and perhaps we must go still further back.

We cannot separate the two belts from the Siberian finds. The Siberian articles were made by artists and artisans of the same school to which the authors of the two belts belonged. They are later, no doubt, and mere repetitions of the same motives. Less force, less imagination are shown, but not yet a decadence. The eagle-yak plaque and the dragon-tiger plaque are full of life and movement. The plaque with the hunt was made by a real artist. It is not a copy, it is an original effort to get away from the conventionalism of ornamental art. Thus, I would suggest, we cannot date the Siberian plaques later than about the first century A.D. This agrees with the date of most of the coins which are supposed to have been found with the Siberian articles. If so, the date of the Novocherkassk find must be approximately the same, or rather a little earlier. The diadem shows some Hellenistic ornamental features (the pendants), which are quite foreign to Roman jewellery.

The animal style as shown in the group of monuments which I have described above differs sharply from the animal style of the Scythian period. The ornamental tendency is the same, but the spirit and the motives are different. The Scythian animal style, while in its prime, adopted the antithetic or heraldic group. It knew the synthetic group, the symplegma of animals. The symplegma was a very common motive in Ionian art, and was very often used by the Ionian artists for adorning articles made for the Scythians. And yet the Scythian artists kept completely aloof from it, although the Ionians, who worked for the Scythians, used it extensively. The new animal style of the Hellenistic and Roman period based all its work on the antithetic and the synthetic group, with a marked preponderance of the latter. The new artists liked the synthetic group, since it gave them such a wonderful opportunity for getting away from the conventionalism and pure ornamentalism of the Scythian art. It allowed them to bring into their creations not only a good bit of naturalism, but also movement and pathos. Their productions breathe the air of vast and dark forests where everything is a constant and fierce struggle. They often saw these battles between animals and they loved to reproduce them. They certainly felt a kind of religious awe at the sight of a ferocious eagle or of a wild tiger. Their imagination populated the mountains and forests not alone with real beasts. The mysterious " tayga " of Asia is full of surprises. Supernatural animals live here as well. But in shaping them, the artists have not invented new fantastic animals. They borrowed the two griffons from the Persians, with whom they had lived in constant contact in the earlier period of their history. But they preferred the dragon : the same dragon which was familiar to the Orient from time immemorial. Now it became the most popular animal along with the fierce eagle-griffon.

Another peculiarity which draws a sharp line between the new animal style and the Scythian one is the polychromy. The Scythian ornamental style had been polychrome in its earlier period, but to a certain extent only. In the fifth and the following centuries its main endeavour was monochrome ornamentalism : to substitute for the plant ornaments the new animal ornaments. The new animal style is thoroughly polychrome, much more so than the archaic Scythian style. The polychromy is the same as we found it in the Sarmatian jewellery. The technique of this polychromy was not invented by the Sarmatians, but borrowed from the Persians. The Siberian torque with the lion griffon shows that the jewels of Persian workmanship were well known to the users of the new animal style. Though borrowed as regards the technical devices the polychromy was developed by the artists of the new animal style on their own lines. It was a heavy and primitive polychromy aiming at producing striking effects. It had apparently been used by the artists for a long time without being subject to outside influences.

And yet there was no complete break with the traditions of Scythian art. There was first of all a common love for the animal theme. Then the bearers of the new style, though retaining the Sarmatian "phalerae" for the horse-bridle, came back in the main to the Scythian solid openwork and relief plaques. In addition, other principles of the Scythian art were kept and cultivated, such as the adornment of animal bodies by other animals and parts of animals, the shaping of extremities as eagle or griffon heads, the ornamental *rôle* of the horns, the horn nimbus (if not the horn palmette), free treatment for ornamental purposes of the bodies of animals.

Who were the creators of this new animal style ? We have seen what the innovations were which the early waves of Sarmatians, who were to a large extent Persianized and Hellenized, brought into South Russia. These tribes had no liking for the animal style. Those who brought with them the new animal style were, on the contrary, fervent admirers of it. At the same time, however, they had the same taste for polychromy and had learned the same technique. They were certainly familiar also with the Scythian animal style. The natural conclusion from these premises would be that the new men belonged to the same family, to the same stock as the first Sarmatians, but inhabited lands further remote from their Hellenized brothers, in the wilderness of forests and mountains.

Such are the conclusions which we have the right to draw from the South Russian and Siberian material. An attempt at a more complete answer to the question of the place of origin of the new animal style and of the nationality of its original bearers will be given in the last chapter of this book.

# NOTES

## CHAPTER II

1. I have dealt with this group of burials repeatedly, the last time in my article: *Sarmatian and Indo-Scythian Antiquities* in *Recueil N. P. Kondakoff*, 1926, p. 239 ff. On the Bobritzkoj Mogilnik and the burials of the Vasjurinskaja Gora see my book *Scythia and the Bosporus*, 1925, p. 493 ff. and 373. On Panaguristshe, B. Filow in *Izvestija of the Bulgarian Archæological Society.* 6, 1916-1918, p. 14 ff. and in *Rôm. Mitth.*, 32, 1917, p. 15 ff. The hook-clasp in South Russia has the form of an eagle-griffon head (the hook), while the flat part of it represents an animal or a part of an animal. It appears first in the burials of Alexandropole (*Antiquités de la Scythie d'Herodote*, PL. I, 3,4 (reindeer) and of Mastjughino (*Compte-rendu de la Comm. Arch. de Russie*, 1905, p. 96, *fig.* 121-122 : griffons with the typical curled noses ; 1906, p. 109 ff. : griffon-boar or griffon-wolf with big tusks and sharp teeth) ; cf. the find of Olbia (*ibid.*, 1901, p. 19, *fig.* 42 : horse). In Central Russia the same type is quite common in the finds of the so-called Ananjino civilization : A. M. Tallgren, *L'époque dite d'Ananjino*, p. 151 ff. ; T. Arné, *National Musei vanners*, 10, p. 165 ff., and so is it also in Siberia, see *Compte-rendu de la Comm. Arch. de Russie*, 1909-1910, p. 231. Compare *Note* 8 of this chapter. The origin of the hook-clasp of the form which has been described above is a difficult problem. A hook-clasp of very similar character, i.e. with the hook in the form of a griffon head and the body consisting of plastic figures of men (or gods, e.g. Herakles) and animals, in round plastic or open-work technique, is typical for almost all the Samnite belts covered with bronze plaques of the fourth and later centuries B.C. The belts being very wide (a substitute for armour) two or three clasps are fastened to each belt (PL. XII, 3 from *Alfedena*). Belts with hook-clasps have been found in almost all the Samnite cemeteries : *Alfedena*, L. Mariani in *Mon. Ant. Linc.* 10 (1900), p. 343 ; F. von Duhn, *Die italische Graeberwelt*, p. 563 ; O. Montelius, *La civilisation primitive en Italie*, 3, PL. 374, Nos 3 and 6 ; *Lanciano* (Frentani), Fr. von Duhn, l.c., p. 604 ; *Cumæ, Mon. Ant. Linc.* 22, 1913 ; *Capua*, many unpublished examples in the local museum ; *Allifæ*, Fr. von Duhn, l.c., p.612 ; *Catanzaro* (Bruttium), etc. ; an interesting set from various places is in the Museum of Naples. Now belts with hooks are quite common in the Italian graves of the early iron period. The most magnificent have been found in the Bernardini and Barberini tombs ; similar ones are in the British Museum (Marshall, *Cat. of the Jewellery*, etc. *in the British Museum*, Nos 1370, 1371). "They are made of silver plated with gold. The body of the clasps consists of more or less complicated frameworks connected by a series of hooks in the center and braces on the sides. The strictly functional portion consists of two similar transverse bars, one of which is furnished with projecting hooks, the other with eyes in which the hooks can engage. From each end of one of the transverse bars projects a pin which engages in a corresponding socket at the extremity of the upper bar. These act as braces... To the outer sides of the transverse bars (away from the hooks and eyes) are attached tapering tubes ending in human heads

and curving upward on one side, downward on the other. " For the Bernardini Tomb. etc. see C. Dinsmoore Curtis, *The Bernardini Tomb*, in *Memoirs of the American Academy in Rome*, VOL. III, 1919, p. 29 ff. Nos 16 and 17, and PL. IX; D. R. MacIver, *Villanovans and Early Etruscan*, 1924, p. 128 ; O. Montelius, l.c, PL. 370, Nos 1 and 2. The transverse bars, of these clasps are adorned with sphinxes, the wire-links which end in the hooks and eyes of No 16 are decorated with human headed birds. On the Barberini clasp see MacIver, l.c., p. 225, *fig.* 67, cf. p. 238. Similar clasps have been recently found at Marsiliana d'Albegna (A. Minto, *Marsiliana d'Albegna*, 1921, PL. XXIV and vignette p. 15). At Marsiliana the ends of the transverse bars in the shape of human, lions', panthers' and horses' heads served as hooks which were fastened to corresponding rings on the opposite side of the belt. Since the style of all the belts described above is the style of the oriental κοινή of the first millenium B.C. there is no doubt that the ornamentation of the hook-clasps was carried out by the artists familiar with this style. It is more difficult to decide whether the form of the clasp also was borrowed from the Orient, e.g. from Asia Minor. The complicated character of the clasp suggests rather the refined Orient than the primitive lands of Central Europe as the place of origin of this form of belt clasp. Another question is whether we have the right to derive the plain clasps of the Samnite graves from the complicated Etruscan originals and whether it is not more reasonable to suppose that in the fifth-fourth centuries B.C. the Ionian Greeks imported both the bronze belt and the hook-clasp for a second time from Asia Minor to Italy. I will come back to this problem in a special memoir.

2. On the early polychrome style in the South Russian jewellery see my book and articles : *Iranians and Greeks*, p. 181 ff. ; *Une trouvaille Greco-Sarmate de Kertch* in *Mon. et Mém. Piot*, 26 (1923) ; *Scythia and the Bosporus*, p. 577 ff.

3. On the Sarmatian *phaleræ* see my article in *Recueil N. P. Kondakoff*, quoted in *Note* 1. In addition to this article I may note that gold and silver vessels adorned with floral motives of the same patterns and in the same style as the vessels of Taxila (comp. *Arch. Survey of India, Ann. Rep.* 1923-1924, p. 61 ff. and PL. XXV, XVXII) and the phaleræ of South Russia are very often found in Eastern Russia and in Siberia : see J. Smirnoff, *L'Argenterie orientale*, PL. XVIII-XX; cf. PL. CXIV, No 286. In the same places also were found bowls and paterae adorned with figures exactly of the same type as the figures on the South Russian phalerae : see especially J. Smirnoff, l.c., PL. XVIII, No 43; PL. XX, No 46; PL. XXXVIII-XL and PL. XCII, CXII, CXIII and CXXV, No 310. Smirnoff has pointed out that all these articles are of North-Indian origin. Some of them bear Pehlvi inscriptions, but according to the late Saleman in a language which is not one of the Iranian languages. It is worthy of note that among the finds made by the Russian expedition in Mongolia there is a circular horse-plaque surrounded by a rope-frame on which a figure of a yak in repoussé work is represented (see PL. XXIV, 5) : comp. my book *Inlaid Bronzes of the Han Dynasty in the possession of C. T. Loo*, Paris, 1927. A large circular plaque with floral ornaments adorns the breast-strap of a horse on a stuff on which some men in Sarmatian dress are represented : see PL. XXIV, 4, and compare Chapter IV of this book.

4. On polychrome jewellery see the books and articles quoted in *Note* 2.

5. See the bibliography in *Note* 2. To Bactria and Northern India the polychrome style of jewellery might have come from the Syrian lands and Egypt and some articles of the new style might have been imported to South Russia from these places. However, the fact that the new style is used for the adornment of articles peculiar to Parthia and South Russia shows by which route the polychrome style arrived in South Russia.

6. The Sarmatians who lived in South Russia for centuries were certainly Iranians; see the book of Vasmer quoted in Chapter I, *Note* 5.

7. On the Yue-chi and the Kushans see *Cambridge History of India*, VOL. I, 1922, p. 563 ff. It is worthy of note that their military dress as shown on their coins was exactly the same as that of the Sarmatians in South Russia, especially the conical helmet; comp. Chapter IV, *Notes* 2 and 14.

8. What use was served by these openwork gold plaques is hard to say. The common opinion regards them as parts of horse-trappings. However, the plaque with the hunting scene shows that the horse-bridles of the bearers of this style were adorned with circular phalerae. The fact that in the two belts (of Maïkop and of Bulgaria) the animal symplegma is used as belt-clasp and that the same motive was used extensively for belt-clasps and belt-plaques in China in the Han period suggests rather the idea that the majority of the Siberian plaques served as clasp-hole pieces for a hook-clasp. (Note that a wide belt is seen on the figures of the hunters, PL. XVI, 2). Against it speaks, however, the fact that the plaques never show either hooks or hook-holes, and that they were intended to be seen from both sides. I would suggest that they adorned the upper part of a quiver or bow-case. There is a great similarity between the famous Siberian eagle and the well known two "fibulae" of the find of Petroasa, see A. Odobesco, *Le Trésor de Petroasa*, VOLS. II, III, p. 67 ff. Still more striking is the similarity between these fibulae and the eagle hook-clasps of Maïkop and Bulgaria. The fibulae of Petroasa cannot be much later than the finds of Maïkop and of Siberia.

9. It is a very long sword indeed, not the short Perso-Scythian *akinakes* of little more than half a metre in length. And such are also those Sarmatian swords which have been discovered in South Russia (about one metre in length; see M. Rostovtzeff, *The Kurgan Finds of the Region of Orenburg of the Early and Late Hellenistic Period* in *Materials for the Archæology of Russia*, 37, 1918, p. 36 ff.), and also the swords which were borrowed by the Panticapaeans of the time of the Roman Empire from their Sarmatian neighbours and kinsmen (M. Rostovtzeff in *Monuments et Mémoires Piot*, 1927, p. 106 ff. and 137 ff.) and of which many examples have been discovered in the Panticapæan graves of this period. Exactly the same form and the same lentgh (1 m. 3 cm.) characterize the swords which have been recently discovered in Chinese graves of the Han period in Korea, see W. Perceval Yetts, in *Burlington Magazine*, VOL. 79, No. 283, October 1926, p. 192 ff., PL. *fig.* E. (the original report of the excavators: Archæological Researches in the Ancient Lolang District, 1925). I have noted in my article in the *Monuments et Mémoires Piot* that one peculiarity of the Chinese swords of the Han period—the use of a special jade plaque—

was equally characteristic of the Sarmatian swords of South Russia. In view of the fact, that, in a Panticapaean grave, a jade plaque of the Chinese type is alleged to have been found fastened to the sword as a guard, I suggested that all the jade plaques of the same form, both in South and East Russia and in China were used for this purpose. Now in Korea the jade plaques of this form have been regularly found fastened to the scabbard of the sword, a little below the guard, and apparently served "as a cleat to hold the scabbard in a leather frog. Possibly the frog resembled that used for our service sword at the present day, and it was suspended from the girdle. " (Yetts). This evidence of the Korean graves is corroborated by the study of the figure of the hunting Sarmatian on the Siberian gold plaque PL. XVI, 2. We see here that the long sword of the horseman hangs on a strap which is fastened to the belt and passes through an object attached to the scabbard of the sword a little below the guard, an object exactly similar to the jade plaques of Russia and China. The other end of the strap was probably fastened to the belt on the other side of the body of the horseman, and the sword thus hung on the strap which certainly was of great advantage to a heavily armed horseman. To the same strap was fastened on the other side (probably by means of another jade) the bow and arrow case of the horseman as seen on the Siberian plaques. In view of this new evidence we must assume with Yetts that either the jade of the Panticapaean sword was fastened to the sword as a guard by the excavators (the find was not made by archaeologists) or that the scabbard-jade was sometimes used as a guard. In every case the evidence shows that the jades in question were first used by the Sarmatians in Central Asia, and came, together with the new type of sword belt, to China and to Panticapaeum. They cannot be a Chinese invention. Cf. my article on this subject in the forthcoming volume in honour of Th. Uspensky.

10. Most of the scholars who have described the hunting plaques of Siberia have compared it with the well known statement of Herodotus (VOL. IV, 22) who, in speaking of the δύρχαι (corrected by some scholars without any reason to τύρχαι) says that the Iyrcae used to kill the animals while seated on tops of trees. A correct description of the plaque which I gave in the text shows that this parallel is wrong. The second hunter climbed the tree, not for spying, but for his own safety.

# CHAPTER III

## THE ORIGIN OF THE SCYTHIAN ANIMAL STYLE AND
## THE ANIMAL STYLE IN CHINA OF THE CHOU DYNASTY

THUS far I have endeavoured to show the gradual evolution of
the animal style in South Russia under the various influences,
which came mostly from Persia, the Southern Caucasus, Ionian
Greece and the Greek colonies on the Northern shores of the Black
Sea. I have distinguished periods in the development of the animal
style and two different aspects of this style : the earlier, which I have
called the Scythian, and the later, which I have called the Sarmatian.
We have seen that this second name is, in fact, hardly correct and
acceptable.

The study of the development of the animal style does not, however,
solve the problem of its origin. The two aspects of the style, the Scythian and the Sarmatian, came to South Russia with all their essential
features. We have not found precedents for these essential features in
South Russia itself. The process of formation of both the Scythian
and the Sarmatian animal styles must have taken place somewhere else.
The question is : where and when ? Let me deal first with the Scythian
animal style.

The first claim to be the home-country of the Scythian animal
style belongs to the lands of the Near East : Assyria, Babylonia and
Phœnicia. The analysis of the animal style of the Near East which I
gave in the Introduction shows however that this style, though
influencing the Scythian style in its early development in South
Russia, does not possess the main features which forced us to assign
to the Scythian animal style its own place in the development of the
animal style in general. The Scythian animal style is more primitive,
more vigorous, less refined than the animal style which reigned in
the Near East in the first millennium B.C.

Next comes Persia. We have seen that the Persians belonged to the same race as the Scythians. Persia for a long time was the neighbour and the rival of Scythia. Many undoubtedly Persian articles were imported into South Russia. Lastly, but not of least importance many motives in the applied arts of Persia, as far as we know them, especially in the toreutics and the jewellery (see especially the Oxus find) coincide with the main motives of the Scythian animal style. However in Persia, even in the Oxus treasure, these motives are exceptional, not dominant as in South Russia. In the main Persia accepted the current Near Eastern animal style without modifying it to any large extent.

Still less founded is the claim of Ionian Greece to be the origin of the Scythian animal style, though many prominent scholars are inclined to explain all the features of the Scythian animal style as modifications of motives peculiar to the Ionian. [1] I cannot accept this explanation. The Ionian animal style is a modification of the Near Eastern animal style, with some peculiarities of rather slight importance. It influenced the development of the Scythian animal style in South Russia in a very large measure. But it cannot explain the main motives of the earliest, the archaic animal style of South Russia. And in its evolution the Ionian animal style showed tendencies which are completely foreign to the Scythian animal style. The Ionians never endeavoured to develop out of the animal motives a special ornamental system. They repeated over and over again some of the creations of the Near Eastern animal style, especially the antithetic and the synthetic groups, and did so especially for the sake of their Scythian customers. There they stopped.

And finally, the Southern Caucasus is, in many respects, closely related to Hittite Asia Minor. It cannot be denied that some articles peculiar to the civilization of the Southern Caucasus in the bronze age appear in the graves of South Russia of the seventh and sixth centuries. It is well known that a peculiar highly geometrized animal style dominated the art of the Central and Southern Caucasus of the late bronze and of the early iron age : engraved figures of men and animals on bronze plaques and on pottery, plastic figures of men and animals on weapons and on various utensils. The stylization of some of the plastic figures, especially of those used as tops of various objects, reminds one of similar figures in the bronze and iron age of Western Siberia (Minussinsk), and vaguely of similar motives in the art of South Russia in the seventh and sixth centuries. But the Caucasian animal style, as a whole, is so peculiar and so elaborate and so dissimilar in its main essence (the geometrizing tendency) to the South Russian animal style, that we cannot but assign a different origin to these two animal styles. The general features of the Caucasian animal style link it up rather with the main features of the animal style of the Hallstatt period in Central Europe. But even with the art of the Hallstatt period there are only a limited number of similarities. [2]

Thus the origin of the Scythian animal style must be sought not in the lands which surround South Russia on the South and on the West. Some coincidences in the Celtic early La-Tène art and the Scythian art of the sixth to the fourth centuries are due probably to the contact between the Celts and the Scythians in the Balkan peninsula and on the Danube. In the main Scythian and the La-Tène style have almost nothing in common. The Scythian animal style certainly came either from the North or from the North-East. The North, i.e. the forests and swamps of Central and Northern Russia, must be eliminated from the outset. Central and Northern Russia in the bronze and in the early iron age show some animal motives in the decoration of the weapons and utensils of their populations. These motives, however, as has been shown by Tallgren and myself, are not original in Central and Northern Russia, but certainly borrowed from the Scythians. A mere glimpse at these articles demonstrates it. [3]

The archaeology of both Siberia and of the adjoining lands of

Central Asia between the Persian and the Chinese Empires is in its infancy. Some good work, however, has been carried out by Russian archæologists in Southern Siberia, especially in the districts of Tomsk and of Yenisei, as far as the Lake Baikal and the Altai mountains. The best studied and the richest district is that of Minussinsk. The museum of Minussinsk is full of articles found both in the graves and in the fields near the town, and there is almost no important archaeological museum in Siberia and in Russia which has not among its treasures some articles from Minussinsk. Many private collections formed at this place migrated to Finland and were scattered to many an European and American museum. Our information is therefore good if not complete. But it bears on a small area only. Outside of this area few systematic excavations were carried out.

At Minussinsk and in other places we must distinguish sharply between the bronze age fully developed and the early iron age. Chronologically, the bronze and early iron age at Minussinsk coincides with the Scythian period in the history of South Russia, especially the early period of the Scythian domination, the sixth and fifth centuries B.C. The general type of civilization is very similar to the Scythian one, especially as regards the arms and weapons. The daggers and the arrows are typically Scythian. The articles, however, which refer to the more peaceful departments of life are not Scythian : they (knives, mirrors, etc.), point either to China as their place of origin, or, which is rather surprising, they show a connection with articles typical of the Southern Caucasus : e.g. the pole-tops ( ?). The horse-trappings are again not Scythian. The type of bridle used in the district of Minussinsk comes to South Russia later, with the Sarmatians.

In the decoration, there is a close coincidence between Minussinsk and South Russia. The animal style plays an important part and it is the same type of the animal style which is so peculiar to the archaic and ripe Scythian period. Rows of animals are used to fill up a space ; beaks and eyes of eagles and eagle-griffons appear as an ornamental motive ; there occur the same stylization of lions, the same crouched or curled position of animal bodies (especially of lions), the same free treatment of the animal bodies (the body being sometime reproduced in a twisted position), the same stylization of the extremities of an animal body. Animals of the Scythian type are used as tops of various objects. Note, e.g. the boar so similar to the well known boar of Alexandropole, the eagle so typical for the Semibratnij Kutgans, and especially the wolf-dragon head. However, there is not the slightest sign of any evolution of the animal style along the lines on which it developed in South Russia. The animal style in Minussinsk is stagnant and limited to a certain few motives.

This shows that Siberia, at least the neighbourhood of Minussinsk, was not the home-land of the Scythian animal style. The animal style penetrated thither from outside together with certain articles, especially the articles of war which, in fact, never have been very popular with the peaceful population of the district of Minussinsk. Had the style penetrated into South Russia from the steppes of Siberia? I can hardly believe it. If it were so, if there were a commercial intercourse between Siberia and South Russia, why should it stop so early ? Why does the animal style of the bronze period in the Minussinsk district look so archaic ? The only solution of the problem is to be found in the hypothesis that the animal style migrated both to South Russia and to Siberia almost at the same time from a common centre. To South Russia it was carried by conquering hordes of nomadic warriors and came therefore in full blossom. It became the style of the ruling aristocracy and throve and developed for some centuries. To Siberia it was imported with the swords and daggers which the Minussinsk people borrowed from their neighbours : the Scythians in the late bronze age. The new animal motives became popular and were used for more than the adornment of arms and weapons. However, the animal style never became the only style of decoration in the region of Minussinsk. Along with the Scythian animal style another animal style, similar to the Caucasian, held its ground, and the ancient geometric style with some new additions (the Celtic scroll) never disappeared completely. [4]

The Siberian material is important since it shows that the origin of the Scythian style must be sought somewhere in Central Asia, in a place from which both South Russia and Siberia could be easily reached. There are plenty of such regions in Central Asia and it is very difficult to point with confidence to one of them. Turkestan has been suggested, [5] but the fauna of the animal style, with its profusion of cervoids, rather points to a land of mountains and forest than to a plain with fertile soil, an age-old region of agriculture. The bearers of the animal style were hunters and nomads, not peasants and agriculturists. They liked the wild animal, the beast, not the tame domesticated animals of an agricultural life. And they were at the same time in touch with the civilized life of the Near East, especially that of the Persian Empire. Some motives of their animal style (e.g. the eagle-griffon) they borrowed certainly from Persia or from peoples subject to Persia.

We must, however, not forget that just at the time when the animal style developed in Central Asia, when it came to South Russia and produced its finest flower, an animal style of a peculiar type was flourishing in China. It is a well known fact that the animal style is the most typical feature of the Chinese art of the Chou dynasty (1125 ?- 250 B.C.). Has this animal style something to do with the Scythian animal style ?.

It is not easy to deal with the Chinese animal style for one who does not know the Chinese language, who has never been to China, and who knows Chinese art therefore not in its natural surroundings, but from articles scattered in the American and European museums. These articles were so often reproduced by Chinese artists centuries after the original had been first created and there is such an enormous amount of deliberate forgeries, that a dilettante like myself has no right to express his own opinion on the date and genuineness of the articles commonly ascribed in the museums to the Chou period. However, for the purpose of this article no such minute analysis is needed. There seems to exist a general agreement on the main features of the ornamental art of the Chou period, and this is what matters and what is essential for our purpose. [6]

The Chinese art of the Chou period is, like the Scythian art of the early period, purely ornamental and much conventionalized. It was mostly in the service of religion, and had, beside the ornamental, a pronounced symbolic character. The idea of the artist was not to reproduce life as he saw it. Even naturalistic animals are rare. His aim is to cover the object which he is adorning with a symphony of ornaments closely connected each with the other. The art is impersonal, more or less communistic and not individualistic. The ornaments which the artists are using are either geometric or animal ornaments. Which system has the precedence we hardly are able to decide. Like the Scythian, the Chinese decorative style is known to us in a highly developed conventionalized form. We have no dated or undated articles which would show the ornamental style in the process of formation. From the earliest times it appears as a mixture of geometric and animal forms, both highly developed and stylized.

Some of the articles are thoroughly geometric in their ornamentation. We are not concerned with them. In the majority, however, the ornamentation is based on animal motives. Full figures of realistic animals are used very rarely. How old the sacred vessels in the form of real or fantastic animals are, I do not dare to decide. The dominating ornamental system consists in taking as the basis of the ornamental decoration of a vase the head or the head-skin of an animal, of covering the friezes of a vessel with rows of animal figures, and in transforming the whole surface of the vessel, all the free spaces, into symphonies of geometric ornaments, with a predilection for the peculiar Chinese maeander or spiral. The most popular animal motives are heads or masks of fantastic animals : (1) The so-called t'ao-t'ieh, or the Chinese ogre mask. It has the form of an animal mask, consisting of a pair of eyes, a pair of ears, two horns and a crest. The animal certainly belongs to the family of felines. I have not the slightest doubt that what is meant is a horned lion-griffon, the most popular animal in the Persian art. (2) The second animal generally used for ornamental purposes is also an old acquaintance of ours. It is the eagle-griffon with all its peculiarities : the large eyes, the curved beak, the ears and the crest. (3) Finally the Chinese dragon — the third animal used by Chinese artists — is beyond doubt the same dragon which we have met so many times, both in the art of the Near East and in the steppes of South Russia and Siberia. I describe here some typical Chinese bronze vessels (see PL. XIX), which show these three types of animals used as ornamental motives.

1. The first is a Ting (boiler for sacrificial food and drink), trilobate, each lobe having the form of an ogre mask with bold, large goat's horns, prominent eyes and flat ears, tusks and nostrils (PL. XIX, 1). The band round the neck is covered by six geometrized dragons in low relief. The legs terminate in heads, which Koop calls dragon heads. The prominent features of these heads are the ears and the crests. (Murray Collection, London ; A. Koop, *Early Chinese Bronzes* : PL. II).

2. A Yu (PL. XIX, 2). The decoration of the body and of the lid consists of very much stylized ogre masks. The handles assume the same form with horns crowned by antlers ( ? ) with an eye in the centre. Friezes of geometrized dragons (Metropolitan Museum of Art ; one of the well known Tuan-Fang sacrificial set. S. C. Bosch-Reitz in *Bulletin of the Metropolitan Museum*, 1924, XIX, p. 144).

3. A typical head of an eagle-griffon is reproduced in relief on the two handles of a Tui (bowl for cereals) ; the ears, the crest, the beak are carefully worked out (PL. XIX, 3). The same handles are

found on a Yi (bowl for sacrificial wine or cereals). The ears of the griffons are shaped here as the beaks and the eyes of an eagle. (Victoria and Albert Museum, London; A. Koop, *Early Chinese Bronzes*, PL. 55, A : cover restored in wood).

4. Bronze carriage mount (axle-cap ?). Note the typical griffon head in relief and the incised t'ao-t'ieh mask (PL. XIX, 4; Philadelphia Museum, with the permission of the director).

Some rather late vessels (but certainly of the Chou type) are especially interesting. One is the well known Yu of the collection of Mrs. E. Meyer, Washington : (PL. XX, 1-3), which I have described and reproduced in my book *Iranians and Greeks*. The lid of the vessel has the shape of a lion-griffon, with all its typical features. The surface of the lid is covered with naturalistic figures of animals (tiger, fish, elephant) on a background of Chinese scrolls. The back of the lid has the same shape of a lion-griffon with horns, which have the form of fishes. The body of the vessel has the form of a standing eagle-griffon with a prominent beak, large eyes, stylized ears and a double crest. The wings are shaped as stylized, almost geometrized, tigers or lions. On the breast of the griffon, another lion-griffon mask. The legs are typical eagle claws. The back part of the vessel represents another lion-griffon head, while the handle is shaped as a tiger head with abnormally large ears. The back legs of the vessel are adorned with human figures. The supports of the handle show the form of human legs. The vessel is such an odd combination of various animal forms that it is not easy to understand or to describe it.

The Yu in the Collection of Mrs. Meyer belongs to a special class of comparatively late Chinese sacrificial vases. The same type is represented by a vase in the Sumitomo collection, which shows the same combination of a lion-griffon lid and an eagle-griffon body (PL. XXI, 2). Similar is another vase in the same collection with beautifully developed wings on the griffon body (PL. XXI, 1). Further variations exist, scattered through Chinese, Japanese, European and American collections.

An interesting though late example of the Chou animal decoration is represented by some vessels of a class of which the most beautiful examples are in the collection of the Chicago Art Institute (PL. XXII, 1, 2); another in the Musée Cernuschi in Paris, and a similar one in the Victoria and Albert Museum at London (Cf. J. Smirnoff, *Argenterie Orientale*, PL. IX, 24, from Siberia). The decoration of the body consists of four interesting animal palmettes. From a lion-griffon's head runs right and left a charming spiral, which consists of two dragon's bodies ending in dragon's heads. These dragons are intertwined with another pair of fantastic animals — this time, eagle-griffons. The heads of the dragons are stylized. The ears show the form of a beak and eye of an eagle.

I may add that the tendency to form animal palmettes is very prominent in the articles of the late Chou period or in articles which in the later periods are using the Chou period system of decoration. The best examples are some bronze handles in the form of an ogre mask. Laufer assigns them to the Chou period, but they might be later. The mask is here transformed into a real animal palmette, the features of the lion-griffon being treated in a purely ornamental way (PL. XIX, 5).

The problem of the origin of the animal style in China is puzzling. The great difficulty consists in the almost complete lack of scientific evidence for dating the Chinese bronzes and the Chinese jades. However, some facts about the early animal style in China seem to be ascertained : (1) The animal style appears in China at once with all its characteristic features, almost without preparation, superimposed on the geometric style of decoration, and partly contributing to its evolution by the geometrization of some animal motives. (2) The animal forms with which the Chinese animal style operates are far from realistic or naturalistic. Realistic figures of animals seldom appear. Whether they are more frequent in the early Chou period or in the late is a question which I am unable to solve. The main animals which are used over and over again are the fantastic animals which I have described above : the ogre mask, the eagle-griffon and the dragon. There might be a difference of opinion on the ogre-mask. In my opinion it cannot be separated from the Mesopotamian lion-griffon whose brother it certainly is. [7] We are on much firmer ground in dealing with the eagle-griffon. There is no doubt whatever that the Chinese eagle-griffon is the Mesopotamian one, with all its peculiar features. [8] And the same is true for the dragon. The Chinese dragon is no more familiar to China than to Mesopotamian, especially Assyrian art, and to the Perso-Ionian art in South Russia. Even the up-turned nose appears very early in the figures of the dragons outside of China. [9]

The main problem of the history of the Chinese animal style is to solve the question of the origin of these three fantastic monsters. Is it possible that the same figures, with the same peculiarities, were invented independently both in the Near and in the Far East ? If not, which region has the priority ? Has the Near East borrowed its fantastic animals from China ? Or vice versa ? As long as we do not know how early these animals are in Chinese art the problem will remain unsolved. In fact, we have no one bronze vase or jade with the animal motives to which we can assign a date earlier than 1500 B.C., a very early date indeed, but much later than many dated Mesopotamian articles with the same animal decoration. However, we must take into consideration that the animal motives appear on all the vases in the same highly conventionalized forms which suggest centuries of previous artistic evolution. Was this evolution carried out in China or outside of China ? Have the Mesopotamian fantastic animals and those of China a common origin ? We do not know.

In my book on the *Iranians and Greeks* I was inclined to accept a common origin, from which both the Chinese and the Scythian animal style were derived. I must say that I was wrong. The real

Scythian style as described above is different if compared with the early Chinese animal style of the Chou period. It is more primitive, more realistic, less conventionalized. It does not operate with fantastic animals. The fantastic animals entered the repertory of the Scythian animal style in South Russia late, probably not before the fifth to fourth centuries B.C. Some features, of course, are common to the Chinese and the Scythian animal style : the use of beaks and eyes as ornaments, the treatment of extremities in a conventional way, the filling of surface on the animals' bodies with figures of other animals, the animal palmettes. However, it seems as if all these features, which are common to the Scythian and to the Chinese animal style, appeared in the Chinese art comparatively late. It is probable that these decorative motives came into China together with some articles of military and funeral equipment borrowed by the Chinese from the Scythian horsemen shortly before the strong Sarmatian influence of which I speak in the next chapter (see PL. XXI, 3, 4, and PL. XXIII).[10]

Thus the early Chinese animal style has almost nothing to do with the early Scythian animal style. It might have come from the same source from which the Mesopotamian animal style was derived, but it had a quite original evolution, and very early assumed forms which were completely alien to the Mesopotamian; for example, the Chinese antithetic group differs from the Mesopotamian type. In general, the Chinese ornamental style of the Chou period has not the same ends and aims as the Mesopotamian, and has a quite different rhythm. A Chinese Chou period vase can be recognized at once. It has its own elaborate and peculiar style, and this style in China has its own and peculiar evolution.

# NOTES

## CHAPTER III

1. B. Farmakovski in *Mat. for the Arch. of Russia*, 34, 1914, p. 32 ff. cf. the Bibliography in Introduction, *Note* 1 of this book and *Iranians and Greeks*, p. 227, *Note* 12.

2. On the Southern Caucasus and its animal style see *Iranians and Greeks*, p. 32, and Bibliography, p. 225, *Note* 5. Compare my Introduction, *Note* 2, and Chapter II, *Note* 4.

3. The articles of A. M. Tallgren on the so-called Ananjino civilization in Central Russia, a civilization which stood under the strongest Scythian influence, are enumerated in *Iranians and Greeks*, p. 228, *Note* 19. Cf. M. Khudjakov, *The Culture of Ananjino*, Kazan, 1922 (in Russian). A new attempt at classifying the antiquities of Minussinsk and at assigning to them more or less exact dates has been made recently by Gero v. Merhart, *Bronzezeit am Jenissei*, 1926. Merhart has not convinced me that most of the daggers of the iron period with their developed animal style belong to the Sarmatian period. I regard most of them as late Scythian, very archaic in their main features. Of great importance are the two volumes of materials published by A. Adrianov, *Excerpts from the Diaries of the Excavations of Barrows in the Minussinsk Region*, Minussinsk, 1902, 1924 (in Russian).

4. The best analysis of the Minussinsk cemeteries and chance finds has been given by A. M. Tallgren, *Collection Tovostine des Antiquités préhistoriques*, 1917, and *Trouvailles isolées Sibériennes préhistoriques au Musée National de Finlande*, 1919. He was the first to divide sharply the Minussinsk antiquities into two groups, and to assign to these groups, which roughly coincide with the Scythian and Sarmatian periods in South Russia, probable dates. In his two books the reader will find a complete bibliography of the subject.

5. e.g. by Tallgren, see preceding *Note*.

6. It is not my purpose to give a full bibliography of books and articles which have been written on the subject of the Chinese art of the Chou period. The earliest works have been carefully registered in the well known book of O. Münsterberg, *Chinesische Kunstgeschichte*, VOL. I, 1910, and VOL. II, 1912. This book is also the best repertory of the Chinese articles which may be dated in the Chou period. Cf. also E. Fenollosa, *Epochs of Chinese and Japanese Art*, 1911, and also S. W. Bushell, *Chinese Art*, 2nd ed., 1909. The best analysis of the Chinese art of the Chou period has been contributed by B. Laufer, especially in his book: *Jade, a Study in Chinese Archaeology and Religion*, 1912 (Field Museum of Natural History, PUBLICATION 154, Anthrop. Series, VOL. X). The methods and aims of the Chinese archaeologists in dealing with the problems of Chinese archaeology and history are illustrated in the excellent article of V. M. Alexeiev, *The Destinies of Chinese Archaeology* in *Izvestija of the Russian Academy of the History of Material Civilization*, 3, 1924, p. 49 ff. The problem of dating the vases and other articles of the Chou period becomes easier after the discovery of some dated finds of early Chinese bronze vases. The most famous find was made recently (1923) in a tomb in Sin-cheng (Honan) and belongs probably to the late Chou period (sixth to fourth century B.C.). The find was a chance find and not all the circumstances of

it are known. The most substantial report may be found in P. Pelliot, *Jades archaiques de Chine*, 1925, p. 28 ff. Whether some jades were found in the same tomb and whether many of the jades which are described as coming from this tomb were really found there remains uncertain. A full bibliography of books and articles which deal with this unique find has been compiled recently by W. Perceval Yetts in *Journ. of the Royal Asiatic Society*, 1926, July, p. 565 ff. Another find is that which was made in 1901, in the territory of Pao-Ki at Tou-chi-t'ai (Shansi), the famous sacrificial table with a set of bronze vases, which is now in the Metropolitan Museum (see S. C. Bosch-Reitz in *Bulletin of the Metropolitan Museum*, 19, 1924, p. 14 ff.; compare P. Pelliot, *Ars Asiatica*, VOL. I., p. 24, *Note* 1), and is commonly ascribed to the late Chou period. A third set found at Shou-ch'un, the last capital of the Chou dynasty, is now in the Boston Museum, see *Bulletin of the Boston Museum of Fine Arts*, 23, 1925, No 138, p. 41; cf. the pair of vases purchased at Yu-ho-chen, *ibid.*, p. 39. By means of the systematic excavations happily begun in China by the Boston Museum let us hope that better information will soon be forthcoming from China and will allow us to come nearer to the solution of many problems in the history of the early Chinese art.

The most important objects of the Chou period are no doubt the bronzes, especially the bronze vases. Many of the richest collections of Chinese bronzes have been recently published and described. (1) The Sumitomo collection at Osaka is no doubt the richest existing collection of early Chinese bronzes. Publication with explanatory notes, by K. Hamada and V. Harada, both in English and Japanese : Sen-Oku-Sei-Shô (Baron Sumitomo, *Old Bronzes*), 6 VOLUMES, 1921. (2) Part of the Imperial collection of the National Museum at Peking (96 bronzes) has been published recently with some bronzes from seven other collections (total 159 pieces) by E. A. Voretzsch, *Altchinesische Bronzen*, 1927. (3) A selection of bronzes which are kept in European, especially English museums (the G. Eumorphopoulos collection and that of the Victoria and Albert Museum) has been published by Albert J. Koop, *Early Chinese Bronzes*, 1927. (4) The early bronzes in possession of C. T. Loo : Tch'ou To-yi, *Bronzes antiques de la Chine appartenant à C. T. Loo* (Préface et notes by P. Pelliot), 1927. Other publications are quoted in G. Migeon, *L'Art Chinois* (*Musée du Louvre*), 1927, and in the article of W. Perceval Yetts, *Literature of Chinese Art* in *Journ. of the R. As. Soc.* 1926, July, p. 561 ff. Compare W. Perceval Yetts, *Chinese Bronzes*, 1925 (extract from the *Burlington Magazine*), and *Chinese Art, An Introductory Review*, etc., *Burlington Magazine Monographs*, 1925. The Early Jades : Gieseler, in *Rev. Arch.*, 1917, p. 127 ff.; Una Pope Hennessy, *Early Chinese Jades*, 1923; P. Pelliot, *Jades archaïques de Chine appartenant à C. T. Loo*, 1925.

7. I have not found any special investigations of the ogre mask in the works which deal with the Chinese art and archaeology. Most of the scholars take it for granted that the type originated in China.

8. The type of the eagle-griffon and its history in China have likewise never been carefully investigated. A Chinese origin is out of the question. A problem, however, arises whether the type of the eagle-griffon is as ancient as that of the ogre mask and whether the so-called

" phœnix " of the Chinese art is a derivation of the eagle-griffon or not.

9. On the dragon see B. Laufer, *Jade*, p. 169 ff., esp. *fig.* 75-90. The dragon (both snake- and wolf-dragon) in the Near East, like the dragon of China, soon becomes a purely ornamental figure, often a sea monster, see e.g. the gold plaque of one of the graves of the tumuli of the Seven Brothers, PL. IX, 2, cf. Rostovtzeff, *Iranians and Greeks*, p. 64, PL. XIII, D (fifth century B.C.). The tail of the dragon of this plaque ends in a duck or goose head, in this respect like so many Hittite fantastic animals of a little earlier time, see Introduction, *Note* 11. Note the upturned nose and the identity of the head of this monster with many heads of the same type found in the graves near the Elisavetinskaja stanitza; see this book PL. XI, 4. There is a striking similarity between the dragons of the Scythians of the fifth-fourth centuries B.C. and those of the Chinese art of the Chou period. A common origin is beyond doubt.

10. I suspect that this is the case of the two jade figures of two small deer with elaborate antlers which have been recently acquired from Mr. C. T. Loo by the Metropolitan Museum. S. C. Bosch-Reitz ascribes them to the Chou period, see *Bulletin of the Metropolitan Museum.* 19, 1924, p. 121, *fig.* Five figurines of the same type are still in the collection of C. T. Loo, see P. Pelliot, *Jades archaïques de Chine appartenant à C. T. Loo*, 1925, PL. XXX. Pelliot is also inclined to date the jades in the late Chou period. However this may be, in this case an influence of the Scythian art is beyond doubt. The treatment of the deer is the same as in so many figurines of deer in the tumuli of the Seven Brothers, those of the Elisavetinskaja stanitza, etc. (see PL. X, XI). There is in the same collection of C. T. Loo a figurine of a deer exactly of the same style in bronze, and many similar figurines were found near Minussinsk; cf. Tallgren, *Collection Tovostine*, PL. IX, 7-8; G. v. Merhart, *Bronzezeit am Jenissei*, 1926, PLS. IV, V, *figs.* 22, 24; PL. IX, *fig.* 3. Scythian influence may be noticed in many jades which are usually dated in the Han period. The best is the figurine of a tiger or a lion with the head turned in the direction opposite to the body; P. Pelliot, *ibid.*, XXIV, 1. It looks as if it were a direct imitation of a Scythian psalion (PL. X, 1). Direct borrowing from the Scythian may be stated for some arms and weapons. Before the Chinese adopted the military equipment of their neighbours in the Han period (see next chapter) they had occasionally used some weapons which had been modelled on Scythian patterns, especially swords and daggers. Two typical Scythian daggers of a pure Scythian shape with a peculiar mixture of Scythian and Chinese ornamental motives are in the collection of C. T. Loo; see PL. XXIII, 2 and 3. On one, along with typical Chinese geometric ornaments on the guard and the handle-top, we see a row of mule-heads in openwork used for the adornment of the handle. The other is adorned exclusively by beaks and eyes of eagles. Some other daggers of the same type are in the Wannieck collection. Another article borrowed from the Scythians is the bell-shaped standard pole. In the same collection of C. T. Loo there is a pair of standard-tops in the form of circular bells surmounted by a typical Scythian figure of a deer (PL. XXI, 2 and 4, cf. PL. XII, 4), parallels to which I have quoted at the beginning of this *Note*. These standards (see next chapter) might belong to the Han period, but their originals are undoubtedly Scythian (see PL. VI, 1 and 2, and

PL. XII, 4). I may mention finally the eye and beak ornament on a javelin head of the Philadelphia Museum, here reproduced with the kind permission of the Director (PL. XXIII, 1).

# CHAPTER IV

### THE ANIMAL STYLE IN CHINA
### IN THE TIME OF THE HAN DYNASTY

I T is a well known fact that in the time of the Han dynasty (206 B.C.-
A.D. 220), which coincides with the Hellenistic period and the
period of the early Roman Empire in the history of the Greco-Roman
West, Chinese life and art underwent a radical change. The stiff,
ritualistic, formal, symbolic, communistic life and art of the Chou
dynasty became more flexible, more individualistic, less traditional
and formal. On the ancient trunk of a tree which had become almost
dry and was beginning to lose its connection with the soil, new
shoots begin to sprout, and, in a very short time, these shoots produce
beautiful leaves and flowers.

One of the most interesting changes which left its traces not only
in the written, but especially in the archaeological documents of this
period is the complete reform of military life and of military equipment. Hard pressed by the Huns and the Yue-chi, the Chinese were
forced to make their archaic army of heavy masses of infantry and
of obsolete war chariots more flexible and more modern, more adapted
to the task of fighting the well organized masses of the heavy and
light cavalry of the Huns and of the Yue-chi. B. Laufer was the first
to point out and to describe this eventful reform. He was the first
also to emphasize that the reform was carried out on patterns which
were of foreign origin. The new military equipment was in the main
that used by the enemies of the Chinese. [1]

The Huns and the Yue-chi were probably Mongolians and Iranians
(or Turks) respectively. But their military equipment and their
military organization they had in common with the Iranian peoples,
who probably had been the first to transform the peculiar features of
the military nomadic life common to all the nomads into a definite
system of organization, tactics, strategy and equipment. We are here

not concerned with the first three items, but the last has an enormous importance for our subject. Let me enumerate briefly some of the most important innovations in the military equipment of the Han period. The flexible scale and later ring armour was first introduced by the Han dynasty; bows and arrows begin to play an important part; the swords and daggers assume new forms, the swords being made very long (1 m., even 1 m. 10 and 1 m. 20), having new forms of sheaths and being worn in a completely new manner. New forms of military banners are introduced, the most curious being a standard with the top in the shape of a circular bell, used both for the army and for funeral processions. Finally new forms of horse-trappings make their first appearance in China : probably stirrups, new forms of bridles with all their accessories, etc. And a new form of military belt is also noticeable : a belt covered with metal plaques and with a peculiar belt-clasp in hook shape.

All these new pieces of equipment have no precedents in the Chinese past, but all are borrowed from outside. Some of them Laufer has shown to come from the Iranian peoples. I can be more precise and affirm that all the innovations in the Chinese military equipment are those which are characteristic of the Sarmatians, as we know them in South Russia. To South Russia, we know, the Sarmatians or the Sakians come from the confines of India. It seems probable that the same innovations or modifications of the ancient Iranian military equipment were taken over by the Mongolians and also the Turks, and through them they penetrated into China.

The ultimate Iranian origin of the equipment is beyond doubt. It is demonstrated by the fact that all the novelties of the Chinese military equipment were brought to South Russia by the Sarmatians, and replaced there the old-fashioned Iranian articles, which had been used by the Scythians. I have proved it in various articles for the scale and ring armour, for the sword and dagger, for the peculiar *porte-épée* by which the swords were loosely fastened to the belt of the heavy armed Sarmatian knights; for the stirrups, for the horse-trappings, which have nothing to do with the Scythian horse-trappings and appear in South Russia for the first time in the third century B.C. — horse-trappings which are so typical of the Parthians and the Sassanian Persians —; and finally for the belts and belt-clasps in hook form, for which I have collected the evidence in Chapter II, *Note* 1. All these articles were probably first used by the Sakians, and afterward, having been modified by the contact of the Sakians with the Greeks, spread far and wide in Asia and in Eastern Europe. Witness for Asia the finds in the Altai and in the Minussinsk region. [2]

As conspicuous as the revolution in the military equipment was the revolution in Chinese art of the Han dynasty. Though still to a large extent symbolical and religious, the art of the Han period is no longer so abstract and so impersonal, so rigid and so formal as in the Chou period. The best instance are the grave sculptures of the Han period, which were collected, dated and minutely described and interpreted by late M. Chavannes. The funeral sculptures of the Han period, though symbolical in their essence, are full of life and movement and highly realistic. The same is true for the glazed and painted funeral clay vases, for the earliest grave terra-cottas and bronzes carefully investigated by Laufer, and also for some articles of other applied arts: bronze bowls and other articles inlaid in gold (beautiful specimens in the collection of Mr. C. T. Loo), jades, etc. The art of the Han period is not a reproduction, a pale copy of some other art. It is national, Chinese in its very essence. However, there is no doubt that it got its new start, its inspiration from outside. Even if we disregard the rather doubtful instance of the Chinese mirrors with their decoration of vine scrolls and realistic animals — they are of a later date — a careful study of the well-dated sculptures, pottery, bronzes and terra-cottas shows a set of new motives which cannot be explained by an organic development of the Chinese art of the Chou dynasty.

The new inspiration certainly came from some sources which were connected with Greek Hellenistic art. The study of movement, the realism, the use of landscape, the introduction of the human figure, the tendency to depict scenes of real life, the love for naturalistic figures of animals : all these features are typical of Greek art in the Hellenistic period. And yet the inspiration did not come directly from Greek sources. The flying gallop, the treatment of the horses, the forms of landscape, the composition, are not Greek. Greek influence came through Iranian hands, and there is more similarity between the Chinese art of the Han period and the Greco-Iranian or the Perso- and Greco-Indian art, than there is with the Hellenistic art of Asia Minor and Syria, not to speak of its western branches. An interesting example of the influence of Greco-Oriental art on the Chinese art of the Han period may be found in the two pairs of belt-clasps acquired in China by Wannieck and Loo, one of which is now in the Metropolitan Museum. The shape is unusual, both for Chinese and for Sarmatian belts; the decoration — Pegasuses running to right and to left — reminds one of the treatment of horses in the Indo-Iranian art of Açoka. Irano-Ionian in its very essence is a circular plaque of the same origin, now in the Metropolitan Museum, showing in the centre a head of a bear and, on the surface of the plaque, two sheep. The plaque recalls the plaques of Vettersfelde, and the comparison of this plaque with a Celtic La-Tène plaque suggested by Bosch-Reitz points to a common Ionian influence.

And yet the art of the Han period remains Chinese. Besides the fact that the articles of the old Chou period are reproduced over and over again, with some stylistic modifications of which I will speak later, we note that the decoration of the tombs and of the glazed pottery also uses extensively, in its symbolical part, the ancient fantastic animals and the decorative motives of the Chou period (e.g. the beak and eye). These are connected into symphonies of animals full of movement and of wild energy. The scenes of the "wild hunt" in the nether world, which are quite common both in the funeral reliefs and on the glazed funeral pottery, are the best instances of the use of the old motives in a new spirit (PL. XXXIII, 2 : a stone lintel of a grave in the Cernuschi Museum in Paris). [3]

There is, however, one aspect of the Chinese art of the Han period which cannot be explained by a Greco-Oriental influence coming from the more or less Hellenized parts of the Irano-Indian area. I mean the development of the animal style in the Chinese art of the Han period. Let me first produce the facts which I have partially quoted in many of my books and articles.

We have seen how a new wave of the animal style swept over large parts of Siberia and went into South Russia, whence it reached Eastern and Central Russia and later the Scandinavian countries and even probably Western Europe, as I have shown elsewhere. This new animal style is pathetic and tragic in its very essence, full of movement and of wild energy in its best productions. It operates partly with traditional motives of the Scythian animal style, but goes far beyond it in using extensively the synthetic groups, the symplegmas of animals, which it probably took over from the Irano-Ionian repertory, infusing the style with new life.

This new style is not confined to Western Siberia and to South Russia. Recent excavations have shown that it has widely spread all over Central Asia. In the region of Minussinsk, the excavations of graves and surface finds showed that the new animal style, which there replaced the Scythian animal style, was closely connected with the appearance of a new form of burial. It is evident that the new style was brought into the region of Minussinsk by a wave of conquerors, who imposed themselves upon the ancient peaceful population of this region. [4] Similar finds in large and well furnished graves were made in the Altai region (see e.g. PL. XXVIII, 8 : wood) ; those of the group of graves of Katanda have been recently carefully investigated and described. [5] Similar graves were excavated in the Transbaikal region, graves which are dated by Chinese coins of the Han period. [6] The same type of grave was also noticed in Western Mongolia, though excavations were never carried out. [7] And finally stray objects of the new animal style went as far as India, where some of them are stored in the Museum of Peshawar (PL. XVIII, 5, 6). [8] From Siberia, the style spread also to the North West. Many an excavation in Eastern Russia especially in the region of Perm have yielded objects similar to those of Western Siberia and Central Asia, and adorned in the same style. [9]

New and very important evidence has been recently disclosed by the Russian scholars Messrs. Kozlov, Teploukhov, Boroffka and their assistants. [10] To the North of the Mongolian capital Urga (about 100 kilometres from this city) and about 10-15 kilometres to the East of the main caravan-road from Kiachta to Kalgan in China, the Russian expedition of Colonel Kozlov found in the mountains of Noin-Ula, in the valleys of Sudzukte and Dzurumte, a set of peculiarly shaped grave-tumuli. Part of these were systematically excavated by Kozlov, and some others by a special archaeological expedition which was sent from St. Petersburg, headed by Messrs. Teploukhov and Boroffka. A full report of this excavation has not yet been published. However, a pamphlet published by the Russian Academy of Science, and articles in the *Illustrated London News* (1925, August 1), the *Burlington Magazine* (by W.P. Yetts), and in *L'Anthropologie* (1925), give me the opportunity of reproducing some of the objects found in these graves and of giving a general characterization of them. The burials in which the finds were made are elaborate constructions, similar to the burials of the same period which are characteristic for the steppes of Orenburg. A rectangular trench was dug deep into the virgin soil with a series of recesses; a corridor on one of the short sides of the trench led to the bottom of the trench, which was then reached by a flight of steps. In the trench an elaborate wooden construction was erected : an outer square pavilion with a flat roof and a smaller second one (inside of the first) in which the wooden coffin was placed. The walls, roofs and floors of the pavillions were covered with beautiful silk and woollen stuffs, and various articles were placed near and in the coffin. The body was buried in state, in rich elaborate dress. Sacrifices were performed after the burial, and remains of the offerings were scattered all over the grave. Then a square tumulus was piled up over the grave. Since all the burials were robbed shortly after the funeral had been carried out, in no one grave were the articles found in their original order and in full.

It is as yet impossible to judge whether all the graves belong to the same time since only a part of the finds has been published. However, it is evident that at least a part of them must be dated in the Han period and is therefore contemporary with the Siberian and South Russian finds which I have described in Chapter II. The general aspect of the civilization which was peculiar to the owners of the graves is nevertheless perfectly evident. The articles which were found in the graves must be divided into three main groups.

1. Some articles (clay vases, wooden lacquer articles, jades, silk carpets and stuffs) show the peculiarities of Chinese art and industry of the Han and of later periods. None belongs to an earlier time recalling the Chinese products of the Chou period. Since the wooden vessels show forms which are not familiar to China and are peculiar to the Scythian and Sarmatian civilization, we may suppose that at least part of these Chinese articles were made for the owners of the graves by Chinese artists or by native artisans trained in the Chinese technique.

2. The second group of articles, especially a part of the woollen stuffs, shows Greek patterns and is worked in the Greek technique (see PL. XXIVA, 1). The style of decoration of these stuffs is the common neo-Ionian orientalized Greek style, perfectly familiar to us from the finds of the Hellenistic period in Syria, Asia Minor and in South

Russia. The question arises how these stuffs came into the hands of the tribe which lived in Northern Mongolia. Boroffka suggests that they came from South Russia. We know that Central Asia, through the so-called Sarmatian tribes, which settled in South Russia, came into touch with the Greek colonies of the Black Sea and carried on an extensive trade with them. Textiles can be easily transported on camels, and there is therefore nothing improbable in the assumption that in exchange for gold, jade, silk, etc., South Russia sent to Central Asia the less bulky Greek wares. However, some of these stuffs show some peculiarities in style and ornamentation which recall Greco-Syrian and Greco-Indian art (to these belong many Oriental, Persian motives foreign to the Greek or Greco-Sarmatian art of the Black Sea), and therefore it may be that they came to Mongolia not from the Black Sea, but from Asia Minor and Syria via Parthia and Bactria. The question cannot be decided as yet. Much will depend on the form and technique of the minor jewellery and on its comparison with the finds of Taxila and the corresponding finds of South Russia. However, the Greek and Hellenistic articles of the Mongolian graves explain for the first time the Hellenistic influence on the Chinese art of the Han period of which I spoke at the beginning of this chapter.

3. The most interesting group of articles which were found in the Mongolian graves is however that which shows a beautiful display of motives of the new animal style of Central Asia, used for the decoration both of textiles and of articles of jewellery and toreutics. Let me describe some of them :

(a) A narrow inset strip of one of the carpets which covered the floor of one of the graves (PL. XXIV, 1, 2). The decoration of this strip consists of two synthetic groups of animals facing each other in the antithetic arrangement and divided by the figure of a stylized tree. The same tree separates the pairs of groups from each other. One group consists of a winged eagle-griffon killing a dying elk. It is obvious that this group imitates or reproduces a metal original : the inset stones are imitated by pieces of material sewn on the stuff of which the bodies of the animals are made. This metal original was of exactly the same type, style and rhythm as the clasps of the Maïkop belt and some of the Siberian plaques. It has the same pathetic and tragic conception, the same savage ferocity. The second group shows a yak fighting with a lion-dragon, in the same scheme which is shown by so many Siberian plaques. The dragon is horned. The extremities of the horns, of the upturned nose and of the tail end in heads of eagle-griffons.

(b) A beautiful fragment of a rug with embroidered figures of three men and three horses (PL. XXIVA, 2). The men wear the typical Iranian costume and head dress. The horses are reproduced with love and understanding, and with a remarkable observation of movement. They are full of life. The horse-trappings are those familiar to us in the Sarmatian graves of South Russia. Prominent also is the big circular breast phalera in repoussé work. The sleeves of the kaftans of the men are embroidered with geometric patterns. The men wear no beards, but have mustaches. The general aspect of them is almost identical with the aspect of the men in the hunting scene of the Siberian plaque (PL. XVI, 2) and with the few figures of Sarmatians which are reproduced on some Sarmatian articles of South Russia. The mustaches and the tuft on the forehead recall the Gandhara sculptures. The fringe of the fragment shows Greek or Greco-Indian patterns.

(c) A gold openwork square plaque (PL. XXIV, 4), with many inset stones. An eagle-griffon and a horned lion-dragon are fighting with a lion. The group is strikingly similar to the Maïkop belt clasp and to the Stockholm plaque (PL. XXVI, 1) ; note especially the position of the eagle-griffon. There is no doubt that the plaque was made by an artist who came from the same school as the artist of the Maïkop belt.

(*d*) A circular metal phalera in the typical rope frame (PL. XXIV, 3). It shows a figure of a yak which stands on the top of mountains and is flanked by two pine trees. It is no doubt a local imitation of the phalerae of Sakian origin, of which I have spoken in an article in the volume in memory of N. Kondakoff (see Chapter II, *Note* 3).

(*e*) An openwork jade plaque (PL. XXXIII, 4) of the same type and the same style as those which are reproduced on the same plate. It shows a heraldic group of two eagle-griffons facing each other. The symphony of these two animals makes a beautiful palmette.

Save for the last article which certainly came from China and shows the strong influence of the new animal style on the art of the Han period of China of which I will speak later in this chapter, the objects which I have reproduced were certainly made, if not by the kin of the buried residents of Mongolia, at least for them and according to their tastes and requirements. The textiles were certainly made by artists trained in the Greek technique : artists who probably came not from China, but either from South Russia or from Indo-Scythia, and the metal articles by artisans who were trained in the same school which produced the Siberian and South Russian objects of the new animal style. We shall investigate later the location of the centre of this school.

Thus it is evident that the new animal style, whatever is its origin, was for a while *the* artistic style of Central Asia. Many recent finds made in Northern China (province of Shensi), the largest part of which have reached Europe and the United States of America by the efforts of Messrs. Wannieck and Loo of Paris, show that the Central Asiatic articles penetrated into Northern China also and were imitated there by native artists. Articles of this type were known to the Chinese archaeologists and were occasionally reproduced in the illustrated works of Chinese scholars. They were recognized long ago as belonging to the well known group of Siberian and South Russian antiquities, of which I spoke above. Some original articles were bought by the Museums and classed with the Chinese antiquities. It is, however, only recently that large quantities of them became known and that it became possible to classify them and to deal with them in the proper way. [11] None of these articles have been found by scholars in scientific excavations. It is obvious, however, that most of them have been found in the graves of Northern China inside and outside of the Chinese wall, some perhaps in Mongolia. [12]

I am indebted to the kindness of Mr. Wannieck and of Mr. Loo for the permission to use their extensive material for the purpose of this book. I am, of course, not able to reproduce all the interesting articles of which I have the photographs supplied by Mr. Wannieck and Mr. Loo. All that I can do in this book is to attempt the first classification of these articles.

A large part of the finds of Mongolia and of Northern China consists of square bronze plaques included in frames and adorned with reliefs or showing flat figures in the openwork technique. Along with these square plaques we have some figures of animals in openwork or groups of animals in the same technique. Most of these plaques were used as belt-clasps corresponding to a hook-clasp on the other side of the belt. Many still show the hole for the hook. Those which have no such holes were probably used as links of a metal belt of which the core consisted of leather. The best examples of complete belts of this form are the Maïkop belt and the belt of the British Museum described in Chapter II. None of these plaques reproduce exactly the articles of the same forms and of the same style of decoration which were found in Siberia and South Russia and are described and reproduced in Chapter II. However, there is no doubt that it is the same school of artisans which made them, and that all of them are coarse imitations in cheap material of articles originally made of gold and adorned with precious stones. Let me reproduce and describe here some of these articles :

Openwork and relief square plaques. One of the most popular motives in the adornment of these plaques is the motive of a wild beast — fantastic or realistic — killing a horse. I have dealt already with the beautiful Maïkop belt-clasp and its counter-part in some of the Siberian gold plaques of the Hermitage, which showed this motive in its most beautiful aspect. The same motive recurs in many variations in a set of Mongolian and Northern Chinese bronze plaques. We see a horse attacked by two wild beasts, the dying horse still naturalistic and pathetic and the beasts highly conventionalized and schematized (PL. XXV, 1, 3).

As popular as the plaques with the dying horse are the plaques which show the typical wolf-dragon alone or fighting a tiger or a horned animal (Yak ?). The Siberian plaque with the symplegma of a dragon and a tiger is well known (PL. XXV, 2, corresp. Konda-koff-Tolstoï, *Antiquités de la Russie Méridionale*, p. 390, *fig.* 350). A curious reproduction of the same group is found on a large plaque of the C. T. Loo collection (PL. XXV, 5). Note that this plaque was never used as a belt plaque. It was nailed in the four corners to a wooden box or some other wooden article (a war chariot ?) of large dimensions. Interesting is also the plaque (C. T. Loo collection) showing a dragon killing a horned animal (buffalo or yak), highly stylized (PL. XXV, 7). The dragon alone, treated on the principles of the Scythian animal style which were partly adopted by the neo-animal style of Central Asia, is one of the most popular figures of the Mongolian and Northern Chinese bronze plaques. I reproduce two examples from the collection of Mr. C. T. Loo, which show the gradual stylization of the motive (PL. XXV, 4, 6).

Other almost exact reproductions of the leading types among the Siberian plaques are quite common in Mongolia and Northern China. Along with the dragon, the eagle and the eagle-griffon is one of the most typical figures of the Siberian plaques. It is represented either with wide spread wings holding an animal in its claws, or fiercely fighting a strong and warlike animal — the yak, the tiger, etc. All these motives reappear in Mongolia and in Northern China. A fragment of a plaque in the C. T. Loo collection (PL. XXVI, 2), is an almost exact reproduction of the Siberian plaque (Kondakoff-Tolstoï, l.c., p. 392, *fig.* 353). It shows an eagle-griffon attacking a tiger and holding in its claws another animal which is also attacked by the tiger. An interesting modification of this motive and a blending of this motive with the motive of an eagle holding an animal in its claws, is seen in an openwork plaque of the Stockholm Museum (PL. XXVI, 1). Two eagle-griffons in heraldic grouping are shown killing an ibex and each holding a hind in its claws. The ibex is reproduced in front view with one head and two bodies or with the body shown from two sides. The scheme is quite common in ancient, especially oriental art, from which it has been taken by the Aegean (Minoan) and the Ionian art. It is quite common, both in South Russia and in India. In South Russia, in the Ionian-Scythian art, the motive was very popular indeed and was used extensively. And whether it was imported to South Russia and India from the Near East, especially from Ionia or belongs to the common stock of Asiatic art, remains to be investigated. [13]

However this may be, the motive of an animal shown from the two sides became one of the favorite motives of the Central Asiatic neo-animal style. I reproduce some of the plaques which show this motive : a mountain goat (PL. XXVII, 1) in a frame which originally was inset with stones, a hare with one head and two bodies (PL. XXVIII, 1), a horse (PL. XXVIII, 5), a camel (PL. XXVIII, 4), a dragon (PL. XXVIII, 2), an eagle with two heads (PL. XXVIII, 3). Sometimes a pair of animals (e.g. two yaks) is reproduced on two plaques, probably of the same belt (PL. XXVIII, 2, 4). Most of the animals are represented in their natural surroundings (forests). The same type of plaques is widely spread all over Siberia, not only in the region of Minussinsk (see e.g.

a plaque with a grazing horse shown in two side-views, *C. R. de la Comm. Imp. Arch.*, 1895, p. 59, *fig.* 137, and another plaque with two yaks in the Hermitage which I reproduce : see on PL. XXVIII, 7). To the same series belongs also the curious belt-clasp (the corresponding part was undoubtedly a hook-clasp) of the Wannieck collection, which takes the form of a curled body of an elk with a wonderfully naturalistic head (PL. XXVIII, 5) : compare a similar clasp of the collection of Mr C. T. Loo (two animals forming one clasp-hole, PL. XXVII, 3). The curled animals, as we know, were one of the best known motives of the Oriental animal style, including in general the Scytho-Ionian.

However, the symplegma, the combination of two fighting animals, remained, along with the motive of a single animal, the most popular motive of the neo-animal style. I reproduce some of these plaques on PL. XXVI, 3 (a griffon and a boar) ; PL. XXVI, 4 (a tiger and a reindeer) ; PL. XXVI, 5 (a highly stylized reindeer surrounded by a kind of halo, a development of its horns). The synthetic and heraldic group of animals shows the same tendency which we noticed for the heraldic group in the Scythian animal style. It gradually develops into a symphony of animals, into an animal palmette. If the Metropolitan Museum gold plaques (one is reproduced on PL. XXIX, 2) which I have reproduced in *Aréthuse*, 1924 (PL. XV, 5; cf. PL. XVI, 1), really come from Siberia, which is very probable, one of them shows unmistakably such a tendency. It is a real symphony of animals, a real animal palmette. The heraldic principle, however, is here organically combined with the synthetic principle and creates a beautiful ornamental rhythm.

The same combination of the heraldic and synthetic groups appears on a curious plaque of the C. T. Loo collection, a real symphony of various animal motives with a peculiar and very interesting rhythm (PL. XXIX, 1). In the centre of the plaque are two crouched stylized saigas in heraldic position. In the four corners four lions with horned heads are biting the necks of the two saigas. To fill up the space between the hindquarters of the lions and the heads of the saigas, a head of another saiga is shown in a front view, its horns being those of the two heraldic saigas. Still more important are two plaques of the same collection, worked in low relief (PL. XXIX, 4). Each shows two tigers symmetrically arranged. The tigers are treated ornamentally in the same way as the so-called hydras which are so typical for the Chinese art of the Han period and are so commonly used by it. I remind the reader of what I have said in dealing with the same motive on the étui-case of Novocherkassk. Note that the principle of composition is no more either heraldic or synthetic or a combination of both. The artist knows both of these principles, but he is using them in a new free spirit. The animals are thrown on the surface of the plaques apparently carelessly, just to fill the space. The arrangement is nevertheless skilful and refined, and reminds one both of the heraldic and synthetic principles, without the rigidity of the first and the ferocity of the second.

Finally, some plaques show the same tendency of reproducing scenes of human life in the forests and woods, which appears also in the Siberian plaques. One plaque in the collection of Wannieck shows two long haired men wrestling in a forest, while their saddled horses are looking at them in amazement (PL. XXIX, 3). I have dealt with this motive in my article in the *Journal des Arts Asiatiques*, and I have mentioned there that the same group of two wrestling men is one of the most familiar groups in the Greek art of Panticapaeum, which endeavoured to portray the military and religious life of the Scythians. The sacred wrestling played probably a prominent part in the rites of the early pre-Zoroastrian Iranian religion.

There is not the slightest doubt that all the articles which I have described and reproduced are not the creation of Chinese artists. They have absolutely nothing in common with the Chinese art of the Chou period and its animal style nor with the neo-Chinese art of the Han period. On the other hand, the art of the Mongolian and

Northern Chinese articles with its peculiar animal style is identical with the art of the gold plaques of Siberia, with that of Mongolia, of the Altai and of the Minussinsk steppes, and with that of the treasure of Novocherkassk and of the related finds of South and Eastern Russia. It is evident therefore that the new animal style was imported into China from Mongolia together with the new articles of military equipment. Many articles of the same type might have been made in Northern China, in imitation of the Mongolian articles, but it was just an imitation or reproduction of motives which were foreign to the Chinese art.

What is the date of our objects? It is a puzzling question. The gradual schematization of some motives (e.g. the dying horse motive) shows that they were in use for a long time. How long, we are not able even to guess, all finds being chance finds. However, it is evident that, in the main, the new animal style of Mongolia cannot be older than the finds of Siberia and South Russia. In these last we notice a real creative genius, we meet with artists who out of some Perso-Ionian motives created a new art and a new style; we witness a strong influence of the classical Greek and Oriental art and an extended use of their technical and ornamental devices (polychromy by means of inset stones). All these features are to a certain extent also characteristic of the recent Mongolian finds in princely graves. However, very little of it can be found in the Chinese articles. They are imitations, not creations, — imitations in cheap material and by mediocre artisans of articles meant to be carried out in one of the precious metals (especially gold) with an extensive use of precious stones.

Even the articles found recently in Mongolia do not show the real flower of the art, although they belong not to common graves of ordinary people, but to graves of great chieftains. Those which have been found thus far are also imitations, better than the Chinese imitations in bronze, but nevertheless imitations. They are therefore certainly later than the earliest and the most brilliant representatives of this art — the Maïkop belt and its contemporary the belt in the British Museum. We have seen that these two belts probably belong to the Hellenistic period — third or rather second century B.C. The finds of Siberia and of Novocherkassk we dated tentatively from the first century B.C. to A.D. the first century. To the same time belong apparently the earliest of the Mongolian and Northern Chinese articles.

The fact of such a wide ramification of the neo-animal style is in itself a very important addition to the history of the animal style. It has, however, a wider bearing. There is no doubt that the neo-animal style of Mongolia profoundly influenced the art of the Han dynasty, and that it was from this source, in connection with the further development of motives of the animal style of the Chou period, that the Chinese animal style of the Han and the later periods sprang up. I speak of the ornamental animal style and not of the realistic sculpture and painting of the Han period with its wonderful study of animals. My thesis is very easy to prove. We have seen that the Chinese in the Han period borrowed from the Huns and from the Yue-chi the essential parts of their military equipment. Some of these borrowings happened to be lasting and became essential parts of the Chinese life for many and many centuries, especially the hook belt-clasp in bronze and jade and the jade adornments of the swords and daggers. Now it is an interesting fact that just these articles display to us an entirely new animal style, more refined and more artistic than the products of the Mongolian art, but based on the same principles and on the same motives. Let me produce some examples.

A. The hook belt-clasps. These clasps appear in Chinese archaeology in various forms (from the plain form, PL. XXX, 2, to the highly complicated of which I speak further on) and in various materials — mostly bronze and jade. Whether these hook clasps were used in the Chou period we do not know. From the Han period on they become quite common. The fact which I have quoted above that the same hook clasp makes its appearance in South Russia with a purely Scythian ornamentation as early as the third century B.C. makes it probable that the form was imported to China from South Russia. The possible suggestion that the hook clasp originated in China and migrated from there to Central Asia and South Russia must be discarded. Very few Chinese articles have been found in South Russia in this early period, and there are no Chinese motives in the early and late Scythian art, none also in the later Sarmatian art. We must assume therefore that the hook clasp came to China with the other parts of the Central Asiatic military equipment in the Han period.

This conclusion is supported by the fact that most of these hook clasps are ornamented in a peculiar animal style. The animals used for this decoration are mostly those common in the art of the Chou period and thus familiar to the Chinese artisans: the lion-griffon, the eagle-griffon, the tiger. Nevertheless some new animals come in, such as the horse, the mountain goat, etc. Still more important is the fact that the artistic treatment of the animals is based on new principles: we have not a juxtaposition of animals or a purely ornamental use of them, but vigorous and pathetic symphonies of animals, synthetic groups, symplegmas, which are entirely foreign to the art of the Chou period. Let me describe some of these clasps.

(1) A clasp in the form of an eagle-griffon, the head forming the hook of the clasp just as in the Maïkop and British Museum belts (PL. XXX, 1, Louvre). The eagle-griffon is ferociously attacked by a winged lion-griffon which bites into its breast. The clasp is a marvellous piece of pathetic sculpture, as vigorous and as wild as the Maïkop and British Museum symplegmas. It probably belongs to the Han period. And yet the motive could not have been invented in China. The symplegma of animals as I have said never appears in the art of the Chou

period, and pathos is unknown to this art. Both features are, however, the outstanding features of the Assyrian and later Perso-Ionian art, from which it was taken and filled with new life by the creators of the neo-animal style of Central Asia. The conclusion is obvious : a Chinese artist took his inspiration from one of the best products of the neo-animal style of Central Asia, probably a belt-clasp similar to the belt-clasp of Maïkop.

(2) A clasp in the form of a highly complicated symplegma of six animals (PL. XXX, 3). A wild tiger or a lion-griffon (note double spiral on its head as a crest), with an elongated winding body, almost snake-like, but with the four lion or tiger paws, has enveloped with the windings of the hind part of its body a dying mountain goat standing upright. Four smaller tigers are biting with ferocious energy into the body of the goat and into that of the larger tiger. Many copies of this clasp are known. The motive was apparently very popular with the Chinese artists. The existing copies might be late reproductions or even modern forgeries or recasts, as Vignier (*Aréthuse*, 1925, April) suggests ; but they undoubtedly reproduce a famous original. Such a symphony of animal motives, so closely connected with the Maïkop belt, the Siberian plaques (especially that of the Metropolitan Museum) and the Chinese plaque which I have described above, cannot be a modern forgery. It is again an imitation by a gifted Chinese artist of one of the best Central Asiatic belt-clasps of the neo-animal style.

(3) Derived from similar Chinese (not Central Asiatic) originals is the charming belt-clasp in the form of an eagle now in the Metropolitan Museum (PL. XXX, 5). The body of the eagle is hollow and is filled by two tigers, commonly called hydras, which form a kind of animal interlace each biting the other's

hind legs. Two splendid eagle-griffons are reproduced in low relief on the inside of the frame.

Innumerable other examples of hook clasps in various metals, partly inlaid with other metals, are known. It is one of the most common Chinese articles. I have no space to describe them in this book.

(4) The same type of belt-clasp has been frequently reproduced in jade. Let me describe two of these jade belt-clasps in the Chicago Field Museum (PL. XXX, 4, 6). Both have the form of a horse with a more or less stylized head. The body of the horse is covered in one of the two clasps by the figure of a tiger with an elongated snake-like body and with a tail which is treated as a plant scroll. On the second, instead of the conventionalized tiger, a splendid realistic monkey is carved. The realistic tendencies of the new Chinese art are gradually taking hold of an originally purely ornamental creation.

(5) A striking parallel to the Chinese hook clasps described above is the gold belt buckle recently discovered in one of the Chinese graves of Korea (PL. XXXIII, 1). The grave belongs certainly to the late first century B.C. The buckle consists of a symphony of dragons and so called hydras (tigers) which is treated in the same style and in the same spirit as are the belt-clasps described above. Note that this buckle is adorned with inset turquoises like the corresponding articles of the Sarmatian art. And yet there is no doubt that the buckle like the lacquers of the same graves was made in an imperial Chinese factory by a Chinese artist.

B. The sword and sword-sheath ornaments in jade. I have dealt with these parts of the military equipment of the Han period in another article (*Mon. et Mém. Piot*, 26, 1923, p. 32 ff. of the reprint; compare above, Chapter II, *Note* 9). It suffices to mention that along with various geometric ornaments of earlier origin, developed in the spirit of the new Han geometric ornamentation with its peculiar " cloud " ornament, the most popular motive of decoration is the same figure of a tiger whose origin is Chinese, but whose treatment is quite new and derived from Central Asiatic originals.

C. To the class of articles borrowed from the northern neighbours of China belongs a large set of bronze buttons sewn on belts, garments and horse-trappings with the ever recurrent decorative motive of a symplegma of animals, mostly a wild beast, complete or abbreviated, biting the head or body of another animal, (e.g. *Aréthuse*, 1924, April, p. 93, *fig.* 23).

D. Let me mention finally a set of objects where animals are used for decorating the top of an object : standards (military and funeral), walking-sticks or sceptres, swords, etc. The standards show a surprising similarity to standard tops in the Caucasus and in the Minussinsk region. They have no strict parallels in the Central Asiatic art of the Hellenistic period either in Mongolia or in South Russia and remind one rather of similar standard tops in Asia Minor and Northern Syria. We have no parallels for these standard tops in South Russia in the Sarmatian period, although similar articles were used in South Russia in the earlier Scythian period. Our evidence, however, is too scanty for affirming that such standard tops were not familiar to the workers in the neo-animal style. The treatment of the animals is full of life and congenial to the principles of the new animal style. The walking-stick tops show mostly the motive of the animal symplegma, and the swords are decorated with animal motives of the Chou period, but treated in the spirit of the neo-animal style (PL. XXXI, 1 and 3 (Sauphar collection) ; 2 (G. Cleveland Morgan collection) ; 4, 5 (C. T. Loo).

The new animal style was not used in China only for the decoration of borrowed articles. Some of the purely Chinese articles, closely con-

nected with the Chinese religious beliefs and with funeral magic, are
decorated in the Han period with the motives or in the spirit of the
neo-animal style. I cannot dwell on this topic at length. Let me produce a few instances. One of the most common features of the Chinese funeral ritual was the habit of giving to the deceased some amulets — square or circular, of bronze or jade. [14] These amulets in
the Chou period sometimes had the form of an animal, e.g. of an
eagle-griffon (PL. XXXII, 7, 9; Chicago, Field Museum). In the Han
period these amulets are still used. Some of them still have the form
of a single animal. But the way in which this animal is treated is new.
The bold figure of a ferocious lion-griffon (PL. XXXII, 2; Sauphar
collection), so surprisingly similar to the griffon of the Maïkop belt, is
not a repetition of a Chou motive. It is a new creation, perhaps of a
later period. And the same must be said of the two similar figures
standing around a symbolical mountain (PL. XXXII, 1, Sauphar collection). However, along with these single figures the new motive
of a symplegma of animals is extensively used. The most popular
symplegma is that of a tiger killing a dying goat (PL. XXXII, 5, Louvre;
cf. 8 and 3, Chicago, Field Museum). Some of these groups may be
considered, as regards their pathos and tragedy, as worthy rivals of
the Maïkop belt-clasp. The spirit at least is the same, and it has no
precedents in earlier Chinese art. Quite different if compared with
these symplegmas are the later not tragic, but idyllic amulets (PL. XXXII,
4, 6).

Less evident is the new influence in the ritual jades which have
been collected and illustrated by Laufer. But even here, with all the
dependence of these objects on the Chou tradition, a new mode of
treatment is easily recognizable. This new mode of treatment is
the same which prevailed in the Han animal style wherever this style
had been used for decorative purposes. Let me introduce some examples. The disc of jade (Ku-pi) published and illustrated by Laufer
(*Jade*, p. 158, *fig.* 71; cf. Rostovtzeff in *Aréthuse*, 1924, p. 11, *fig.* 22)

is covered with the so-called grain ornament. On the edge the disc is surrounded by an openwork frame which consists of three animals. In the centre is an eagle-griffon facing left with head to right. The tail and the crest are treated as plant scrolls, the ends of these scrolls having the form of beaks and eyes of an eagle. Two horned dragons are crawling from both sides towards the griffon. The dragons are treated ornamentally in the same way as the tigers of the Han period, usually called hydras. The bodies are snake-like, agile and full of movement, the real nature of the lions' bodies being emphasized by the paws ; the heads are very large with open mouths and the typical upturned scroll-like noses. The extremities of the dragons are transformed into plant scrolls, with the beak and eye motive extensively used. These scrolls unite in the back of the figures in a real palmette, thus completing the openwork frame. The decoration is charming. Nothing remains of the wild ferocity of the Central Asiatic animals. And yet the symmetrical heraldic composition, the treatment of the bodies, the expressiveness of the figures, the beak and eye motive must be ascribed to the new impulse which has been given to Chinese art by the animal style of Central Asia. I reproduce on PL. XXXIII, 3 and 5 two charming openwork amulets of the above described type. One of the Sirén collection (Rostovtzeff in *Journ. d. Arts. As.*, 1924, p. 16, *fig.* 1) shows two dragons in a heraldic position facing each other, their bodies being transformed into a symphony of quasivegetal scrolls, which rest on a charming figure of a butterfly with wings spread. The other (Field Museum) is adorned with two figures of tigers (so-called hydras) whose bodies end in rich scrolls of vegetal appearance but of animal origin. It is sufficient to remind the reader of the animal palmettes of the late Scythian period (see PL. XI), to make him realize the far reaching similarity between the two sets of monuments. And yet there probably existed no direct borrowing in China from the late Scythian source. Exactly the same features are conspicuous in the jade openwork palmette found in one of the

Mongolian graves which were opened by the Russian expedition (PL. XXXIII, 4).

To the same impulse must be ascribed the symbolical animal symphonies of the funeral sculptures and of the funeral pottery of the Han period of which I have spoken above (PL. XXXIII, 2, Musée Cernuschi). While the realistic motives can hardly be derived from the Northern Central Asiatic influence (though realistic motives, as we have seen above, are not unfamiliar to this art), the wild symphonies of fantastic animals hunting and chasing the deceased man's soul and each other, are quite new in their combination and not at all familiar to the Hellenized Iranian art, from which the Han period realism was probably derived. The general treatment of these figures, the purely ornamental and highly unnatural position of the bodies of the animals, the combination of animals in one uninterrupted animal symphony, the motive of animals biting each other's tails or fighting each other, the extensive use of the beak and eye motive, and the general similarity of the treatment of the animals to that which we have already met in the various articles produced by the Chinese art of the Han period : all this allows me to think that here we have another example of the influence, on Chinese art, of the art of Northern Central Asia with its highly developed animal style.

I cannot dwell on the further development of Chinese art. The animal style has not disappeared from Chinese art down to our time. It was and is extensively used for ornamental purposes. And even in its latest offshoots it has not lost the most marked features which point to its foreign origin. The Chinese animal style remains what it had been in the Han period — a Chinese version of the Northern Central Asiatic animal style. I have, of course, not exhausted all the problems which are connected with the main problem of the origin of the new Chinese art of the Han period. My aim was not to solve these problems. For such a task my equipment is not sufficient. What I have endeavoured to show is that with the Han dynasty a large quantity of foreign articles was imported into China. They came first with the foreign soldiers and later, when the Chinese army was reformed on new lines, were adopted by the Chinese soldiers as parts of their new military equipment. No doubt that Chinese artisans began to make them on foreign patterns, and in doing so gradually modified their forms and ornamentation.

The ornamental motives which were used in adorning foreign articles and which were thus reproduced and modified by the Chinese artisans were all of them animal motives in various and often fantastic combinations. Not one of these animal motives belongs exactly to the group of motives which formed the stock of animal motives used and developed by the Scythian animal style. Some are similar, but the spirit in which they are treated is entirely new. It was a new animal style. Its main features I have described above. About its origin I am going to speak presently.

In China, to which quantities of new articles decorated in the new animal style were imported, the new animal style had a great success. We must not forget that the animal style was traditional in China and that the animal motives were extensively used by Chinese artists. Thus once introduced into China the new animal style firmly established itself in this country. The Chinese artists were, however, so gifted and so highly trained technically that as soon as they adopted the new animal motives and the new mode of their treatment, they began to modify them. The wild and ferocious energy, the far reaching pathos of the style, first eagerly reproduced by the Chinese, were gradually reduced and softened. What they learned from their northern teachers was to treat the animals in connected groups, synthetic or antithetic, to study more closely the body of the animal and to infuse movement and expression into the representation of animals. The wild energy disappeared, but life and movement remained in the gracious and elegant figures of animals, which originally were taken over by the Chinese from their northern and western nomadic neighbours.

I have endeavoured in the preceding pages to characterize the new animal style and to describe its history and development both in the East and in the West. I have stated many times that not one of the areas, where the articles which were carried out in this style were found, may claim as yet to be the place of origin, the home of this style. It is easy to say that the style certainly originated somewhere in Central Asia. However, Central Asia is a very large place and a very vague location. Can we aspire, as things stand now, to more precision? Can we point out a special place which has more reason than any other to take on itself the honour of being the home-land of the new style?

It is obvious that the style is a new development of some motives and forms which are peculiar to the Greco-Oriental art. The synthetic and antithetic groups, the symphony of animals, the treatment of the animals, the technique of metalwork and the polychromy were all borrowed, not invented or created by the artists who used the new animal style. Their originality consists in something else, which I explained on the previous pages. From whom did they borrow all the elements which they have so extensively used? I think that I have proved that it was not Scythian art which supplied the artists with these elements. And it was also not the pure Greek neo-Ionian art. It was this art, but with the admixture of some foreign Oriental elements. All this I have shown in my second chapter and I concluded from this and from some other considerations that the creators of the new animal style were not the Sakians, the first waves of Sarmatians who came to South Russia, but some of their neighbours, residents of mountains and forests, hunters and warriors, men who had not lost direct contact with nature, who loved, feared and worshipped the animals.

Where these neighbours of the semi-Hellenized Sakians lived is not easy to say. The fact that the yak is one of their favourite animals seems to point to Tibet and the adjacent countries, the home of the yak. However, we know so little of the Tibet of this period, of its ethnography and history, to insist upon this point. Scientific excavations in Tibet may solve the problem.

Wherever the home of the new animal style might have been, it is obvious that it suited the tastes of many peoples in Central Asia and that it was adopted by almost all those who had a real importance in the history of Central Asia of this period. Of these we know two groups : the so-called Yue-chi and the Huns. If the original home of the Yue-chi was Tibet, they may claim the honour of having created the new animal style. In any case they certainly adopted it and carried it with them far and wide on their extensive military expeditions and migrations. We know that just at the time when the new animal style spread so widely, the Yue-chi, under the pressure of the Huns, moved gradually from the confines of China westwards, conquered Northern India and Turkestan and probably also large parts of Siberia. If not the inventors, the Yue-chi were certainly the carriers of the new animal style, and it is probably the Yue-chi who brought this style to South Russia. [15] Whether the Huns took this style from the Yue-chi or from a common source is difficult to say. They were certainly not the inventors of the style. When they later came to South Russia and to Europe the style was already there.

I have finished the task which I have set for myself in this book. I have followed the Scythian and the " Sarmatian, " i.e. the Central Asiatic animal style in its gradual development. We saw how closely connected was the Scythian style with the other animal styles — that of the Near East and that of China. It received many impulses from the animal style of the Near East, and in its turn may have had some influence on the early Chinese animal style of the Chou period. But for the development of the Oriental, Greek and Roman classical art, the Central Asiatic animal style in its early Scythian form had no importance whatever. Classical art ignored it, and it existed as a mere provincial art of a border-land which took over some elements of the classical civilization.

Far more important was the new form of the Central Asiatic animal style, that to which I have applied the name of Sarmatian, but which in fact must be rather connected with the Yue-chi. This art remodelled the Scythian animal style on new lines. Its artistic and technical inspiration it took from the Irano-Ionian animal style, but infused in this style, which at that time (about the third century B.C.) had become highly conventionalized, a new life and a new force. This new animal style possessed what the old Scythian style had completely lacked — the force of imposing itself, of influencing other arts, of spreading far and wide. It spread in its original form all over Central Asia, Siberia and South Russia; it penetrated into China and influenced one of the aspects of the Chinese art of the Han period; from South Russia and Siberia it entered Central, Eastern and Northern Russia and created here, in the Roman imperial period, a curious offshoot of highly conventionalized animal style. Finally, from Russia or through Russia, the new animal style reached the Scandinavian lands and created, as I firmly believe, the amazing flower of the animal style in the early mediaeval art of Sweden and Norway.

It is not my task to follow this movement of the animal style northward and into Central Europe. Other scholars can do it much better than myself. Nor can I do more than ask the question whether this animal style influenced the Byzantine and early Russian art. In itself, this episode in the history of art is interesting enough to justify my endeavour to follow its destinies through the ages.

# NOTES

## CHAPTER IV

1. B. Laufer, *Chinese Pottery in the Han Dynasty*, 1909; *idem, Chinese Clay-Figures*, part 1, *Prolegomena on the History of Defensive Armour*, 1914; *idem, Sino-Iranica, Chinese Contributions to the History of Civilization in Ancient Iran*, 1919. Prof. P. Pelliott dates the beginning of the new age in China about a century earlier, see Toung-Pao, 1925-1926, p. 265.

2. The general aspect of an Iranian heavily armed mounted hoplite is familiar to us from the frescoes in some of the graves of the Roman period in Kerch and from Parthian and Sassanian sculptures. The equipment of these late Iranian knights has very little in common with the equipment of the Persian soldiers of the Achæmenian period and with that of the Scythians. The same equipment, however, recurs in the figures of mounted warriors which are often carved on the rocks of Siberia on the banks of the river Jenissei. They have been often reproduced, e.g. by Laufer, *Chinese Clay-Figures*, p. 222, *fig.* 35. Note the " tamga " (family sign) on the croup of the horse similar to those which are so common on the Sarmatian and Greco-Sarmatian antiquities, especially on belts and cauldrons. These horsemen are probably the Yue-chi or the Huns. Almost identical with the Sarmatian and Siberian military equipment is that of the Kushan kings in Northern India (ring and scale armour, conical scale-helmet), see A. Foucher, *L'art greco-bouddhique du Gandhara*, 1918, VOL. II, PL. C, 15 and 17; compare Chapter II, *Note* 3. In addition to the suggestions of Laufer I may quote some new facts, which I collected in my books and articles. The scale and ring armour so typical for the Chinese of the Han period, are both found in the graves of the Sarmatians on the Kuban river. The typical trilateral arrow-heads of the Scythians and Sarmatians are common in China in the Han period as shown by the examples in the Field Museum. Stirrups were found, both in China (PL. XXIII, 4; of the Han period? Comp. P. Pelliott, *l.c.*, p. 261, *Note* 1) and in the Sarmatian graves of the Caucasus (according to a definite statement of the late Professor N. Vesselovsky who has excavated the graves. I must add that I have not seen the stirrups in question. I have no doubt, however, that an archaeologist of the experience of Vesselovsky could not have committed a mistake. This in answer to the statement of Prof. P. Pelliot, *l.c.*, p. 262, *Note* 2). The swords and the daggers are almost identical in China of the Han period and in the Sarmatian graves of South Russia, both in the Caucasus and at Panticapaeum (see Chapter II, *Note* 9). The same jade ornaments were used in both places as scabbard jades (see Chapter II, *Note* 9). Finally the whole set of horse-trappings of the Chinese as shown in the monuments, both of the Han and later periods is neo-Iranian and so are also the Sassanian horse-trappings. Sarmatian (borrowed from the Scythians, see Chapter III, *Note* 10) seems also to be the use of bells as military and funeral standard tops (see PL. XXI, 2 and 4). On all these topics see my books : *Iranians and Greeks*, p. 129 ff. the Panticapaean frescoes, p. 162, PL. XXIX), and *Scythia and the Bosphorus*, p. 559 ff.;

cf. my articles in *Mon. et Mém. Piot*, 26 (1923), in *Materials for the Arch. of Russia*, 37 (1918) and in the forthcoming volume in honour of T. Uspensky ; cf. Pelliot, *Jades archaïques de Chine appartenant à C. T. Loo*, 1925, PL. XLII and description. The typical Asiatic cauldrons which are familiar both to the Scythians and to the Sarmatians in South Russia, and are found both in East Russia, Siberia and China and as far as Hungary, ought to be collected in full and subdivided according to their corresponding dates some of them are as early as the sixth century B.C., some as late as fifth-sixth century A.D. The last article on these cauldrons has been contributed by Z. von Takacs in the *Izvestija of the Bulgarian Arch. Inst.*, 3, 1925, p. 205 ff. (with good bibliography). On the hook clasps in China see B. Laufer, *Jade*, p. 262 ff.

3. On the Chinese art of the Han period see my book *Inlaid Bronzes of the Han Dynasty*, 1927, where the reader will find a bibliography and an analysis of the various artistic currents of this period. The belt-clasps of the Perso-Ionian-Indian art have been published by S. C. Bosch-Reitz, *Bulletin of the Metropolitan Museum*, 19, 1927, p. 296 ff. Another pair of belt-clasps with the Pegasus are in the Wannieck collection. The circular plaque of the Metropolitan Museum shows close connection with some articles in the Oxus treasure (Dalton, *The Oxus Treasure*, 2nd. 1926, Nos 25 ff., esp. No 37) and with some earlier articles on the Vettersfelde find.

4. Among the finds of the area of Minussinsk there is a group of iron age graves which certainly belong to some conquerors who probably came from the East, and which show great similarity to the finds of Katanda, Mongolia and China of which I am going to speak presently and those of Western Siberia and South Russia of which I spoke in CHAPTER II of this book. See A. M. Tallgren, *Collection Tovostine*, p. 18 ff. To this period belongs certainly the plaque illustrated by A. M. Tallgren, l.c., PL. IX, No 16, and also probably the button-like bronzes PL. IX, Nos 19-20. The article on PL. VI, 1, of the same publication, is the Chinese Ch'i-ling, a jingle for a banner ; see A. Koop, *Early Chinese Bronzes*, PL. XLIII, *e*. Many other articles of the same time are also of Chinese origin which shows that the conquerors of the Minussinsk area lived for a long time on the confines of China. As I have pointed out in Chapter III, *Note 4*, G. v. Merhart in his recent book *Bronzezeit am Jenissei*, goes too far in assigning to this period almost all of the iron age stray finds of the Minussinsk area. Some of his parallels (see especially PLS. X, XI and XII) however are convincing. I was not able to consult the recent accounts of excavations in the Minussinsk area and in the Altai district by Teplukhov and Rudnev, respectively, in *Materials for the Ethnography of Russia*, 1927, VOL. III, p. 2 (in Russian).

5. The finds of Katanda which were made years ago by late V. Radloff have been recently republished in full and illustrated by A. Zakharov, *The Antiquities of Katanda*, in *Journ. of the Royal Anthropological Inst.*, 55, 1925, p. 37 ff. The decoration of some of the articles shows the same predilection for the synthetic group of fighting animals and survivals of the Scythian animal style. Typical of these finds is also the tendency towards a realistic reproduction of animals, especially horses which show the greatest similarities with the horses as reproduced on the two Siberian plaques portraying scenes in the lives of the

owners of these plaques (see PL. XVI, of this book). An interesting group of wooden and bone articles from Katanda of the animal style have been recently published by the same author in *The Antiquaries Journal*, 1926, VOL. VII, p. 410 ff; of great importance is the fact that the horn cheek-pieces reproduced on p. 414, *figs*. 8, 9 are degenerate reproductions of some Scythian objects of the fifth century B.C. of which I speak on p. 19 (PL. VII, 7).

6. Talko Grintzevich, *The Prehistoric Cemetery of Sudja in the Ilmova Valley*, in the *Works of the Troitzko-Savsk and Kiakhta Section of the Priamur Branch of the Russian Geographic Society* 1, 2 (1897) and in the *Proceedings of the Twelfth Archaeological Congress at Kharkoff in* 1902, 1, p. 482 ff.

7. Grano, in *Journal de la Société Finno-Ougrienne*, 26 and 28 : reports on archaeological expeditions to South Siberia and West Mongolia for 1906, 1907 and 1909.

8. A chance find in India, now in the Peshawar Museum, shows an unmistakable relation to the Siberian and South Russian gold articles of the new animal style of which I spoke in Chapter II of this book. One is a gold figurine of a stag, another a gold openwork armlet which shows a symphony of animals (dragons with upturned noses) biting each other's tails (PL. XVIII, 5 and 6). The frame of the armlet and the joints, ears, eyes, etc. of the animals were originally adorned with inlaid stones in the typical Siberian technique. See *Arch. Survey of India, Ann. Rep.*, 1919-1920, PL. XXIV, *b.* and *c.*

9. In Eastern Russia articles similar to those which are characteristic for the Sarmatian period in South Russia and for the civilization of which the most marked feature is the new animal style are commonly found on some places for sacrifices in the region of Perm. The civilization of these " Kostishcha" (bone-heaps) follows chronologically that of Ananjino and belongs to the period from the first century B.C. to the fourth century A.D. This civilization is commonly called that of Pianobor or of Gladenovo, places where the most important finds have been made. See A. A. Spizyn, *Antiquities of the Chud of the Kama ; idem, The Kostishche of Gladenovo*, in *Zapiski of the Russian Arch. Society*, VOL. XII, p. 1 ; *idem, The Shaman Figures*, in *Zapiski of the Russ. Section of the Russ. Arch. Soc.*, VOL. III, p. 1 (1906) ; A. M. Tallgren, *La civilization dite d'Ananjino*, p. 183 ff. ; *idem, Den Yral-Altaiska Arkeologins Upgifter*, in *Finsk Tidskrift*, 86, 1919, p. 271 ff. ; *idem, L'Orient et l'Occident dans l'âge du fer Finno-Ougrien* in *Journ. de la Soc. Finlandaise d'Archéologie*, 35, 1924. A. M. Tallgren pointed out that on these sacrificial places were found the same scabbard jades which are characteristic both for Sarmatian South Russia and China of the Han period (see Tallgren, *L'Orient et l'Occident dans l'age du fer*, p. 23 of the reprint). Note that the only coins which were found at Gladenovo were coins of the Kushans and of the Indo-Parthian kings (Kadphizes I, A.D. 45 or 50-85) and Gondopharnes, the well known Indo-Parthian contemporary of the Kushans, see V. A. Smith, *Catalogue of the Coins of the Indian Museum*, Calcutta, 1906, p. 65 ff. and p. 54 ff. (the coin of Gondopharnes with the inscription Sasasa is generally attributed to a king Sasan, who probably never existed). Among other articles found in the region of these " bone-heaps " a curious hollow bronze statuette of a rider was recently discovered, a statuette which served as vessel for libations (the upper part of the head of the rider serves as the lid of the vessel) ; see A. V. Schmidt in

*Zapiski of the Collegium of Orientalists*, VOL. I, p. 429 ff. Schmidt is right in regarding this statuette as a product of the Central-Asiatic art, but is wrong in dating it in the sixth-seventh centuries A.D. The statuette belongs certainly in the second or third century A.D. and came to Russia from Northern India. I have showed this in a special article where I have published a similar statuette now in the collection of Mrs. John D. Rockefeller (in the *Mon. et Mém. Piot*, 28, 1925-1926, p. 164 ff.). Cf. my article, *Le Dieu Cavalier dans la Russie Meridionale, en Indo-Scythie et en Chine*, in *Seminarium Kondakovianum*, 1927, VOL. I, p. 147 ff. (in Russian).

10. " Short account of the expeditions for the investigation of Northern Mongolia in connection with the Mongolo-Tibetan expedition of P. K. Kozlov, " Leningrad, 1925 (especially the three first articles of P. K. Kozlov — general report, geography, flora and fauna ; S. A. Teploukhov—account of the excavation of the barrow No. 24; and G. I. Boroffka — on the finds from the historical point of view ; also a short account of W. Perceval Yetts in the *Burlington Magazine*, April 1926, based on the Russian report with reproduction of all the important articles found in the grave ; compare also his article in *Journal Royal As. Soc.*, 1926, p. 555 ff.; cf. the figured silks excavated recently by Sir Aurel Stein, in the *Burlington Magazine*, 1920, July-September. Cf. also G. Boroffka's *Griechische Stickereien aus der Mongolei* in *Die Antike*, 1927, VOL. III, p. 64 ff., and *Die Funde der Expedition Koslow* in *Arch. Ang.*, 1926, p. 341 ff., and on the Chinese silk stuffs found in South Russia, N. P. Toll in *Seminarium Kondakovianum*, 1927, VOL. I, p. 85 ff. I am sorry that I am forced to reproduce on my plates some of the illustrations of the Russian pamphlet without a special permission of the Russian Academy of Sciences and before the final publication of the finds. However, the finds are too important for the subject which I treat in this book and a mere reference to the pamphlet or to the article of Yetts would be utterly inadequate.

11. The first to point out the similarities between the Chinese and the Scythian life and art in general was P. Reinecke in *Zeitschrift f. Ethn.*, 28, 1896, p. 1 ff. On Reinecke's suggestions are based the superficial and vague remarks of Münsterberg, *Gesch. der Chin. Kunst*, I, p. 36 ff. S. Reinach, *Représentation du galop*, 2nd ed., p. 80 f. and E. H. Minns, *Scythians and Greeks*, p. 280, were the first to quote some illustrations in the Chinese Atlases which reproduce some of the " Mongolian " plaques of some Chinese collections. The first Mongolian articles were bought by the British Museum and the Metropolitan Museum of New York. See Sir Hercules Read in *Man*, 1917, p. 1 ff., PL. A, and S. C. Bosch-Reitz in *Bulletin of the Metropolitan Museum*, 1918, p. 135 ff. Compare H. d'Ardenne de Tizac, in *Rev. de l'Art ancien et moderne*, 43, 1922, p. 81 ff. ; *idem*, *Les Animaux dans l'Art Chinois*, 1923. I have dealt with this subject repeatedly ; see *Iranians and Greeks*, p. 203 ff.; *Aréthuse*, 1924, p. 81 ff., and *Revue des Arts Asiatiques*, VOL. I, 1924, p. 11 ff ; cf. the fine set mostly of the Eumorfopoulos collection published by A. J. Koop, *Ancient Chinese Bronzes*, PL. 108-110, and U. Pope-Hennessy, *Early Chinese Jades*, PL. XXI, 2 ; cf. *Rev. d. Arts Asiat.*, I, 1924, p. 14.

12. As regards the origin of the articles of which I am speaking in this chapter I have received

ample and excellent information from Mr. L. Wannieck. In his letter from Peking dated the 7th of January, 1925, he writes as follows : *D'abord je tiens à confirmer qu'aucun objet n'a été trouvé par moi personnellement. A Tchuloohsien* (Chülu-hsien) *j'ai assisté aux fouilles faites par les indigènes et je leur ai acheté les pièces sortant de terre. Dans les villes détruites du Toumed j'ai ramassé par terre les débris des porcelaines dont j'ai fait cadeau aux différents Musées, mais j'ai également acheté les pièces intactes des paysans des villages établis en dehors des villes. Par contre il n'est pas juste que j'aie acheté toutes les pièces scythes de marchands venant de Mongolie.* In describing his journeys in quest of the so-called Scytho-Chinese bronzes Mr. Wannieck mentions that he bought the first articles at Peking (March, 1923). Then he went on his journey with the intention of going to Ninghsia and Kansu through the region which lies to the North of the bend of the Yellow River. His first station was Kwei-hua-ch'eng, then Paot'u and To-sheng-tzù. In all these places he bought the bronzes from local travelling antiquarians, the Ta-lor. Back in Peking he acquired some bronzes from people who come from Yü-Lin-Fu and from Si-an-Fu (Shensi). From this report it is evident that the bronzes are found mostly in Mongolia and in Northern China, but are also scattered far and wide all over N. China. In full accord with the statement of Mr. Wannieck is the information which I received from Mr. C. T. Loo. Most of the " Scythian " bronzes in his collection have been found or purchased also at Yü-Lin-Fu and at Si-an-Fu in the province of Shensi.

13. On the motive of the double (or multiple) animal with one head in Indian art see Ananda K. Coomaraswamy in *Ostasiatische Zeitschrift*, VOL. II, (1913-1914), p. 383 ff. cf. *idem, Catalogue of the Indian Collections in the Boston Musuem of Fine Arts*, VOL. V (Rajput Paintings), 26-50 PL. DCLVI. Mr. Coomaraswamy quotes in his last publication two early examples of this motive in Indian art. One is the two lions with one head on a railing pillar of the Sunga period (2nd century B.C.) at Garhawa (Cunningham in *Arch. Surv., Ann. Rep.,* VOL. 10, PL. V), another consists of four deer with one head at Ajanta, Cave I (decorative relief on a capital). I am indebted to Mr. Coomaraswamy for the communication of the proofs of his Catalogue. On Minoan and Ionian monuments with this motive, see Murray, *Journ. Hell. Studies,* 1881, p. 318, and K. Friis Johansen, *Les Vases Sicyoniens,* 1923, p. 131 ff. On the evolution of the motive in general in Oriental and Greek art, see S. Reinach in *Anthropologie,* 1895, VOL. VII, p. 655 ff., 699 ff.; R. Zahn in *Anatolian Studies presented to Sir William Ramsay,* 1923, p. 442 ff; Valentin Müller in *Orientalische Literaturzeitung,* 1925, p. 785 ff.

14. B. Laufer, *Jade,* PL. XL.

15. The nationality of the Yue-chi is still a matter of controversy, cf. Chapter II, *Note 7.* Their racial type as shown on the coins of the Kushans seems not to be Iranian, though no exact study of this point has ever been carried out. But their dress, their military equipment, their horse-trappings are similar to, or identical with those of the Sarmatians as we know them from the South Russian monuments. Moreover the gods of the Kushans as represented on their coins have been shown to bear Iranian (pre-Zoroastrian or Zoroastrian) names and to express in the forms which they have assumed on the Kushan coins Iranian and to

a small extent Indian religious ideas in a Greek travesty, see M. A. Stein in *Babylonian and Oriental Record*, VOL. I, 1886-1887, p. 155 ff., and A. Cunningham, *ibid.*, VOL. II, 1887-1888, p. 40 ff.; cf. also C. de Harlez, *ibid.*, VOL. I, p. 206 ff., and E. W. West, *ibid.*, VOL. II, p. 233 ff. I do not know whether any article of importance has been written since on the subject of the Kushan religion. We do not know the language of the Kushans as their written documents in India are in Kharoshti (script derived from the Aramaean; the language is an Indian dialect) and the inscriptions on their coins partly Kharoshti, partly Greek. There is a strong presumption therefore in favour of the Yue-chi being either themselves Iranians or having lived for a long time in contact with and under the influence of the Iranians and having adopted entirely their religion and civilization. It might be that the Kushan kings belonged to a Turkish tribe which ruled over a set of partly Turkish, partly Iranian tribes (cf. the similar case of the Mitanni and of the Hittites).

PLATE I

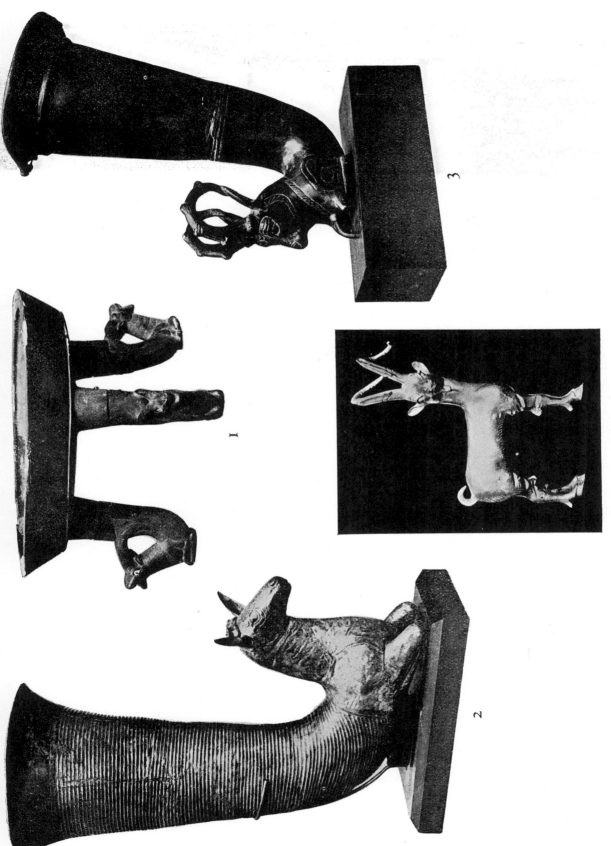

PLATE II

PLATE III

1

2

PLATE IV

1

2

3

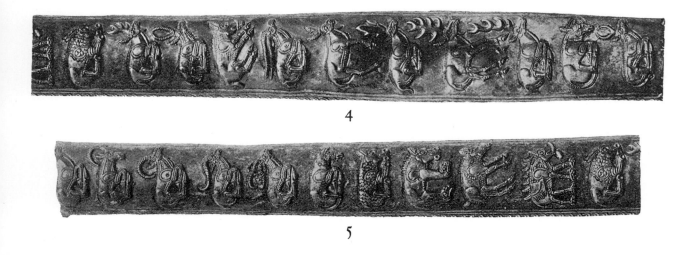

4

5

PLATE V

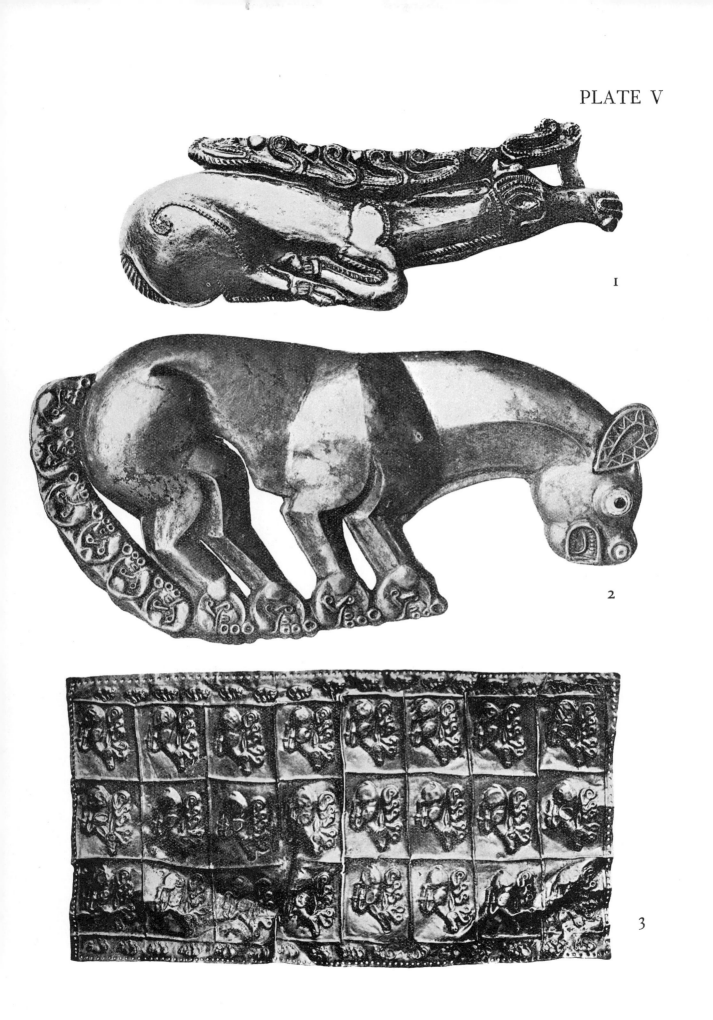

1

2

3

PLATE VI

1

2

3

5

4

PLATE VII

1 — 4

5

6

7

PLATE VIII

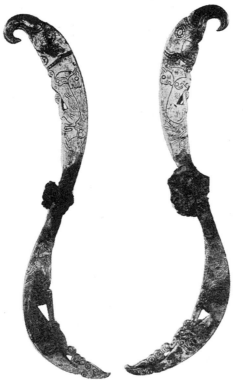

1

2

3

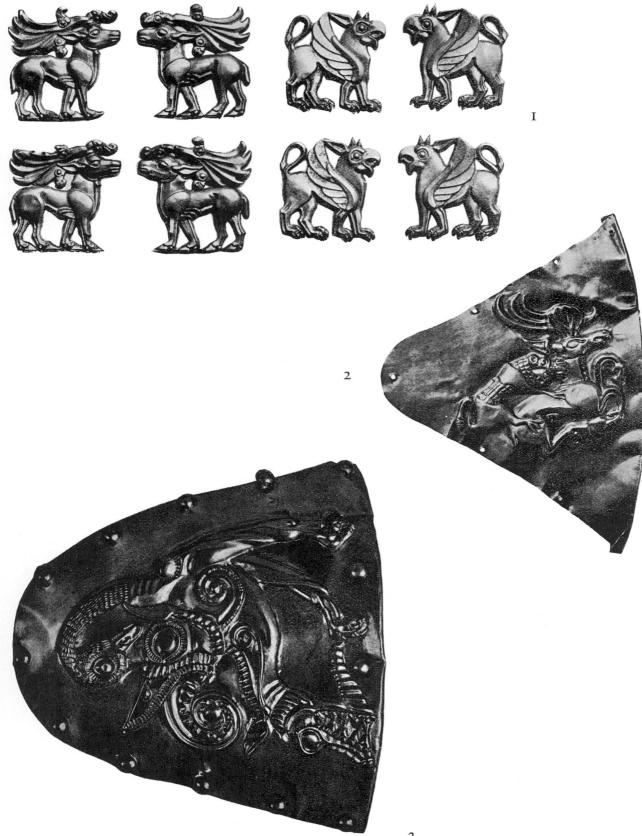

PLATE IX

1

2

3

PLATE X

1

2

3

4

5

6

8

7

PLATE XI

PLATE XII

1

2

3

4

PLATE XIII

1

2

3

PLATE XIV

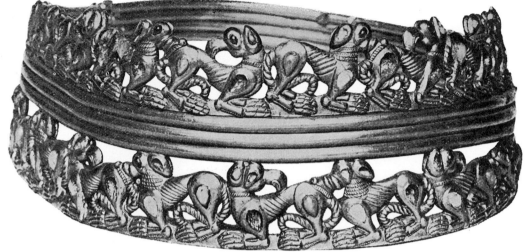

1

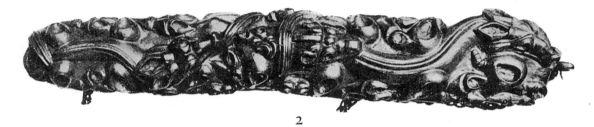

2

3

4

5

PLATE XV

1

2

3

PLATE XVI

1

2

PLATE XVII

I

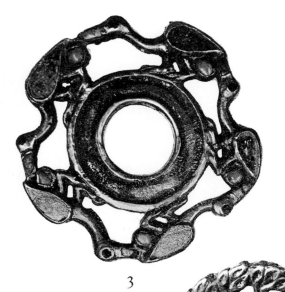

3

4

2

PLATE XVIII

1

2

3

4

5

6

PLATE XIX

1

2

3

4

5

PLATE XX

1

2

3

PLATE XXI

1

2

3

4

PLATE XXII

I

PLATE XXIII

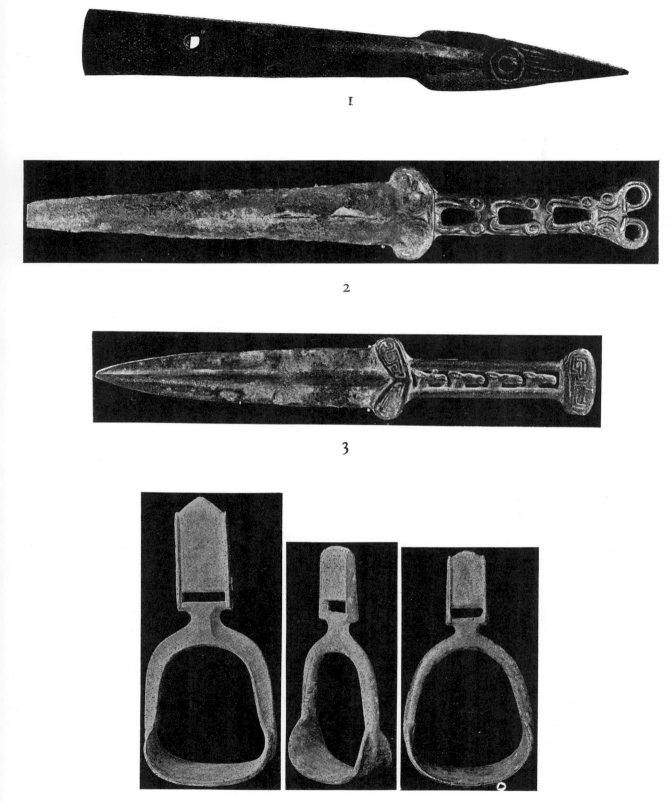

1

2

3

4

PLATE XXIV

PLATE XXIV A

I

2

PLATE XXV

1

2

3

5

6

4

7

PLATE XXVI

1

3

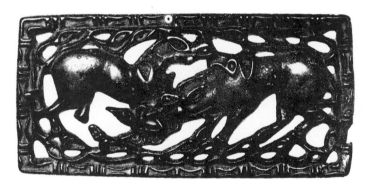

2

4

5

PLATE XXVII

1

2

3

4

5

PLATE XXIX

1

2

3

4

PLATE XXX

1

2

3

6

5

4

PLATE XXXI

1

2

3

4

5

6

PLATE XXXII

I

2

3

4

5

6

7

9

8

PLATE XXXIII

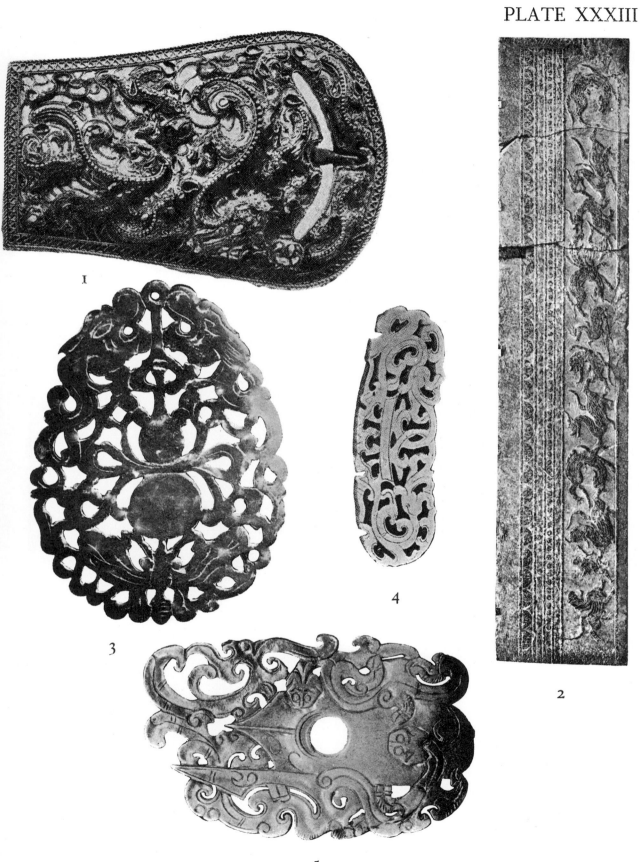

1

3

4

2

5

*Printed in U.S.A. by*
NOBLE OFFSET PRINTERS, INC.
NEW YORK, N.Y. 10003